Neues Museum Berlin

Neues Museum Berlin

by David Chipperfield Architects

in collaboration with Julian Harrap

photography by Candida Höfer

essays by
Kenneth Frampton, Julian Harrap, Jonathan Keates, Rik Nys,
Joseph Rykwert, Karsten Schubert, Peter-Klaus Schuster, Thomas Weski

and a conversation between
David Chipperfield and Wolfgang Wolters

edited by
Rik Nys and Martin Reichert

Verlag der Buchhandlung Walther König

Contents

Preface

As part of the sequence of high-quality projects made in recent years, David Chipperfield has now concluded the rehabilitation of the Neues Museum. The rigour of this work is testament to a long process, intense dialogue and extensive participation. These are intimately related tasks which frequently fail to be addressed in today's architecture.

Chipperfield's intervention includes different and complementary options: integrated restoration; restoration that maintains the marks of time and Berlin's history; and reconstruction.

These three attitudes correspond to different problems posed in the rehabilitation of Friedrich Stüler's project. The building presented a state of decay which nevertheless preserved the essence of the volumes, the spaces, and the finishes. Some of these were restored with exemplary integrity. In others, Chipperfield's sensibility yielded, in a coolly calculated way, to the painful beauty of the ruins, as if consolidating instantly a timeless latent process of decay.

The demolished north-west wing and south-east corner would necessarily have to be reconstructed. There the architecture of Chipperfield emerges, as if it had always existed and could not be otherwise; neither reproduction nor opportunistic branding by the author.

These different attitudes, intersecting here and there, constitute the essence of the strategy for a project that is, I believe, one of the most consequential lessons in architecture from the last decades. With the complex history of the building and its architectonic expression recovered, the Neues Museum stands as a crucial reference for the construction of Berlin.

Álvaro Siza

The project for the reconstruction of the Neues Museum lies outside the normal circumstances of an architectural realisation. Throughout the process it was not clear how the project related to our usual concerns and skills. We convinced ourselves to see this project as unique and beyond our ordinary practice, both organisationally and intellectually; conventional methodologies were abandoned in favour of processes and procedures adopted specifically during the course of the project.

And yet, emerging finally from this extraordinary and privileged process, we may reflect that we have been immersed in the most intense way in the profound territory of architecture, territory that is so often reduced or sacrificed in the typical professional process.

At a time when the planning and realisation of architecture is continuously compromised in its rigour by the impatience of commercial pressure and by the reluctance of the building industry to pursue quality, when the virtual seems to have more influence than the physical, and when the desire for effect and image has replaced the discussion of meaning, the project for the Neues Museum placed us in the most intense contemplation of architecture.

The subject of restoration and reconstruction tends to provoke a high level of emotional and intellectual debate. Nowhere have these issues been articulated so well as in Germany. The discussions of the post-war years, dealing with the debris of cities and monuments, were once again revisited with the reunification of Germany in 1989/90; in no other city was the subject more seriously debated than in the newly unified Berlin.

The physical and conceptual constraints that we set ourselves with our approach to reconstruction created challenges both technical and intellectual. The finished building is a testament to the skills and professional commitment both of the planning team and of the craftsmen and contractors who realised the project. However, the real privilege resided in the climate of debate and discussion that surrounded the project and became a fundamental part of its process. While some of the opposition seemed at times ill-informed, prejudices and emotions should not be lightly dismissed. As architects, we demand that the public be more interested in their environment, and we cannot complain when they betray the emotions that they attach to the buildings of their city. Indeed, it is this intensity of ownership that has infused the project with so much meaning. It is a tribute to the citizens of Berlin that they have engaged so thoroughly with the process and with the result.

Our vision was not to make a memorial to destruction, nor to create a historical reproduction, but to protect and make sense of the extraordinary ruin and remains that survived not only the destruction of the war but also the physical erosion of the last 60 years.

This concern led us to create a new building from the remains of the old, a new building that neither celebrates nor hides its history but includes it. A new building that was made of fragments or parts of the old, but once again conspiring to a completeness. Where each decision, whether about repair, completion or addition, was grounded by the articulation of its physical quality and its meaning, where all parts of the building attempt to inflect to a singular idea; an idea not of what is lost, but what is saved.

David Chipperfield

Photography by Candida Höfer

February and August 2009

The Museum Rejuvenated

Joseph Rykwert

Any house – even a hut – you build embodies a history, that of its own building. For a public institution, the actual business of building may have a complicated backlog of debates and even quarrels that have shaped it. After it is built, time will alter and modify it, year by year. Every overlay or intrusion will add to or disturb its patination.

The Neues Museum has passed through more history in its century and a half than most buildings. When August Stüler designed it, he was relatively young, at the outset of a successful career, the favoured pupil and assistant of the great Schinkel. The new building he proposed was to stand adjoining (and at right angles to) his teacher's masterpiece, which thus became the Old or Altes Museum, whose Ionic colonnade affirmed Berlin's claim to be the new Athens. And he connected the two with a bridge over the street (now Bodestraße), as if with an umbilical cord.

The Neues Museum was to be the first portion of Stüler's and the Prussian king's larger plan for what is Museum Island, now designated a World Heritage Site. Frederick William IV, the 'enthroned romantic', inherited the Prussian Kingdom in 1840; he had studied architecture with Schinkel, and as a draughtsman he was both fluent and visionary. It was very much part of his plan for the capital that the northern part of the Spree island extending from the Palace and the *Lustgarten* should become the new spiritual and intellectual centre of his realm, a forum sheltered from the worldly bustle of Unter den Linden. It was to incorporate academies, the new university and a Cathedral (which was built much later, but on the east side of the *Lustgarten*) with a *Campo Santo* for the monuments of Prussian royalty and other worthies. The stately colonnade of Schinkel's Altes Museum would be a frontispiece for this ensemble.

Meanwhile, that Museum had been filled to overflowing. The post-Napoleonic frenzy for accumulating works of art, mostly from the Mediterranean, stimulated a competition for primacy among princes and governments, and Prussia was at its forefront. Where original masterpieces were not to be had, plaster casts would have to make do. By 1841 the need for more space prompted various proposals. Schinkel had died that year and the king inevitably chose his natural successor, Stüler, to trace the outlines of that majestic forum and to design the Museum. Its first instalment was a Doric stoa which was to link its future buildings.

Taking the Doric columns of that stoa as his base, Stüler designed a tripartite structure over it: the ground floor of his building took up the proportions of the colonnades, while the main storey was Ionic, the attic Corinthian. So far it followed the conventional superposition of the orders.

Above: Sketch of Museum Island by Frederick William IV, showing high central temple.
Pencil on paper, ca. 1840.
Below: Cross-section of the south wing of the Neues Museum with the Greek Courtyard.
Lithograph from: F.A. Stüler, *Das Neue Museum in Berlin*, Ernst & Korn, Berlin 1862, plate 10.

But the way the exhibits were organised within that space also suggested another kind of tri-partition – that division into the symbolic, the classical and the romantic periods which formed the evolutionary account of human history expounded in G.W.F. Hegel's famous lectures on aesthetics that he had given during the 1820s in Berlin but which were not published until after his death in 1835. It is doubtful if Stüler, who was no theorist, was aware of such speculations. Frederick William IV for his part may have detested Hegel, but the grand historical scheme was widely discussed and seductive; it would certainly have been well-known to others involved in conceiving the museum's direction.

That is why the prehistoric and early history rooms, the ethnographic collection and the Egyptian section with its miniature of the Ramesseum in West Thebes, whose glass roof turned it into a solemn court, were at ground level, as was the Historic Hall in the north-west corner, whose ceiling was supported by proto-Doric columns based on those at the Beni Hasan tombs. The construction details and surface finishes harmonised with the ordering. At this level the roof is vaulted and solid, and the floors are of terrazzo. The Ionic *piano nobile*, on the other hand, has marble columns based on those of the Erechtheion porch (Stüler had been the draughtsman for Schinkel's project for a Greek Royal Palace on the Athenian Acropolis), while its floors are mosaic. Some of the long galleries are roofed in a novel manner: segmental cast-iron flat arches dictate the curve of the vault and are braced by straight wrought-iron tie-beams that take up the sideways thrust of the vault. Stüler filled the arcs with filigree figures and ornaments in zinc and brass. The top storey had wooden floors and slender cast-iron supports decoratively clad in die-cast zinc; it accommodated the *Kupferstichkabinett*, the principal collection of prints and drawings, and a Gothically vaulted chamber, the *Sternensaal*, for the mediaeval relics from the royal Hohenzollern art cabinet.

The building was also tripartite in plan: the collections were housed in the long wings, each with an internal courtyard, while the dominant centre of the building was the vast monumental staircase, its tallest element, which rose above the gallery roofs into sculptured pediments. The north and south ends of the eastern façade – the one towards the future forum – were completed by two domed corner pavilions whose cornices were supported by five caryatids each.

Work on the building, which had progressed smoothly until 1848, stalled when the Revolution broke out, with which the King sympathised at first, though he took fright when he realised its implications. That same year, the Frankfurt Parliament offered him the Imperial crown, but he rejected it – he would 'not pick it out of the gutter'. And although he hesitated to restore order in Berlin by calling in the troops, his treasury was depleted by the events and work stopped for a while.

Still, the King was an active participant in the assembly of the museum interiors. The visitor was introduced through the Doric, vaulted galleries into the staircase hall: as you rose to the principal and classically designed main storey, you passed between casts of the monumental (5.6 m high) Dioscuri, the twin horse tamers from Quirinal Hill in Rome, fancifully attributed to Praxiteles and Pheidias, and ordered by the King. On turning round at the landing, you looked up at the summit of the stairway to a replica of the caryatid porch from the Athenian Erechtheion, which was originally surrounded by a blind arcade of Corinthian pilasters.

About the time of the Revolution, the King invited the Munich history painter Wilhelm von Kaulbach to provide the visitor ascending the stair with an overwhelming panoramic vision of all human history and achievement: it was to be the climax of the museum. Kaulbach was a disciple of the same Peter von Cornelius who had decorated the Glyptothek in Munich and had, a decade earlier, moved to Berlin to paint the frescoes for the proposed *Campo Santo* (which was not to be). He was not well received and in the end only executed Schinkel's panorama of human progress in the portico of the Altes Museum – just completed at the time. Kaulbach's early fame as the 'German Hogarth' had been diverted by his ambition to paint history: 'We must paint only history! History is the religion of our times! Only history is contemporary!' he was quoted as commanding.[1]

The whole panorama of human history was therefore summarised in six panels, each 7.5 m long, separated and framed by decorative adjuncts, mostly in grisaille. The subject of each panel was much discussed. Kaulbach decided to begin with the first historical act, the fall of the Tower of Babel – in accordance with the vision of the history of human freedom held by his Munich friend Friedrich Wilhelm Schelling, who had also moved to Berlin in 1841 and was an opponent of Hegel. The cycle culminated in a complex Reformation scene, a group of many figures surrounding Luther holding up his Bible.

Kaulbach took from 1848 to 1866 to paint the panels, using the laborious novel technique of stereochromy (or mineral painting) directly on the plaster. The panorama became his best-known work, and for a while enjoyed greater fame than the building that housed it. It was much discussed and published, and both emulated and caricatured. The paintings were completely destroyed in the 1943 bombing. Only the cartoons for them survive.

Kaulbach was by far the most famous of the many artists involved in painting the building's interior. Decorative and stage painters provided each hall with landscapes and historical scenes to create an appropriate setting for the exhibits: Northern mythology, the woodlands of Rügen Island and the shores of the Baltic Sea were the subjects at ground level – along with the much more popular Egyptian themes – while higher up there followed views of Greece, Rome and Italy. Each room was in turn divided into three horizontal zones: the dado and the monochrome walls gave the exhibits a restful background, while the upper sections and the ceiling (notably the ultramarine, elaborately patterned one of the Hall of Mythology suggested by the father of German Egyptology, Richard Lepsius) were given over to the various decorators.

1 'Geschichte sollen wir malen! Geschichte ist die Religion unserer Zeit! Geschichte allein ist zeitgemäß!' In Cornelius Gurlitt, *Die Deutsche Kunst seit 1800* (4th ed.), Berlin 1924, p. 215.

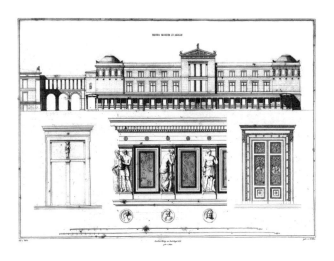

Above: East façade of the Neues Museum looking toward the colonnade courtyard with the connecting bridge to the Altes Museum and details of the main portal, the windows of the *piano nobile* and the risalit figures. Lithograph from: F.A. Stüler, *Das Neue Museum in Berlin*, Ernst & Korn, Berlin 1862, detail of plate 5.
Below: Perspectival view of the Egyptian Courtyard. Lithograph from: F.A. Stüler, *Das Neue Museum in Berlin*, Ernst & Korn, Berlin 1862, plate 7.

Above: Photograph of the Staircase Hall looking west with the plaster casts of the Dioscuri (between 1916 and 1943).
Below: Unrolled original cartoon by Wilhelm von Kaulbach for the mural *The Age of Reformation* in the Alte Nationalgalerie.

The King's project for a high, apsed, temple-like building which was to dominate the proposed forum was revived towards the end of his life. Stüler was engaged to develop and interpret the royal sketches, but by then he was withdrawing from directing the Neues Museum works, which he handed over after 1854 to his fellow Schinkel pupil and assistant, Friedrich Adler. Stüler had other important commissions, such as the National Museum in Stockholm. Dying childless in 1861, the King was succeeded by his brother William I, who would be proclaimed Emperor ten years later. The project was now taken over by Johann Heinrich Strack, yet another Schinkel pupil, and he developed it in a much more ornate and sumptuous – incipiently Wilhelminian – manner. When the connoisseur and collector Gustav Waagen died in 1868, leaving his collection to the nation on condition it was given an appropriate building, the destiny of the royal project was sealed and it became the National Gallery (today the Old National Gallery).

The rapid growth of the Berlin collections required further expansion. Much of the Oriental and newly acquired European art was given its own building, the Kaiser Friedrich (now Bode, after its first director) Museum on the northern tip of the island. Between it and the Neues Museum Alfred Messel built the rigidly classicist Pergamon Museum (which is dominated by its vast exhibits as the Neues Museum never was and is to be restored according to designs by Oswald Mathias Ungers) to house the vast finds from that city, as well as the Ishtar gate from Babylon, so completing the Museum Island that is today a UNESCO World Heritage Site.

When the Neues Museum was adapted for the rather different museography of the 1920s, most of the plaster casts were moved out and the decorative operatic frescoes on the walls panelled over, while the ceilings with their elaborate figure paintings were concealed by plain suspended ones. Paradoxically, these surface coverings were peeled off during the shoring-up work of the late 1980s, and the highly decorative interiors have reappeared from underneath them; they bear not only the scars of war damage, but also others inflicted by the anchors from which the lower ceilings had been hung. Bombs and piecemeal repairs thus put paid to the *sachlich* re-surfacing and revealed the more colourful ornament of the original interiors. From the Revolution of 1848 to the destruction of 1943/45, accidents of history have buffeted the Neues Museum, while the philosophers' vision that moulded its original conception and dictated its ordering no longer speaks to many of us, shattered as it was by the very same events. History as a grand narrative, as it originally shaped the Neues Museum or informed Kaulbach's vast paintings, no longer corresponds to the way we order our past – which is much more fragmentary, much more concerned with the particular, with micro-histories, with strife and conflict, rather than an epic account of the progression from one epoch to another. That may be why a renewal of the sixfold panorama could not be realistically considered. Even if some way could be found to replace the paintings with replicas of the surviving cartoons, those flaccid and balletic groups of figures would no longer dance for us. Our eyes could not take them in as late-19th-century eyes once did.

This involves a larger issue – that of the protection versus the restoration of historical buildings, a question that has been much debated and even legislated since the mid-19th century. To restore an imperfect building to a supposed once perfect state implies the restorers' superiority to its fallible builders, while an attempt to return it to its 'original' condition suggests that the building has not had a history – or that whatever history it had can be 'cut off' at some arbitrary point in time, that there is some state (which must always be a hypothetical one) to which the building can revert.

In the case of the Neues Museum, a decision would therefore have to be taken as to whether it was to be restored to its condition in 1930 (with its neutral museography) or to its 1866 state, when Kaulbach had finished the stereochrome frescoes and the scaffolding was finally removed from the stairway; or even to the project as Stüler first conceived it, with his blind Corinthian pilaster arcades taking the place of the vanished panoramas – which would, of course, have emphasised the vertiginous height of the hall.

Put this way, any such alternatives may seem unacceptable. Even simply repairing the exterior is not a straightforward proposition, as during the wartime catastrophe large areas of stucco fell off the walls. Should what remains be stripped and the whole building be uniformly replastered – or should it be merely patched up? Should the breaks between the surviving old and new stucco be smoothed over or should they be emphasised? And what of the cracked caryatids on the domed corner pavilions of the eastern façade? And the *putti* built into the stone window frames? There is no way, in any case, to adapt any such approach consistently to both the interior and exterior of this building.

Chipperfield has taken on the challenge frontally: he has chosen to accept all the marks and scars of the building, all the layerings that have taken it from Schinkelian sobriety through Wilhelminian opulence and Weimar *Sachlichkeit* to end in the raging horrors of the Second World War, so that the renewed building can stand as a witness to all of its past, shelling and bombing scars, bullet holes and all. Whatever has survived has been retained. The sculptures do not hide their wounds. Those walls that were stripped bare have been tinted and shaded using slurries and glazes, and where the bricks needed completion, local historical ones have been reused. The mosaic and the terrazzo floors have been patched up and smoothed to be serviceable again. The fragments have been gathered so that nothing that survives is lost. The staircase hall in particular had to take on a new role, since Kaulbach's panoramas and the Erechtheion caryatids were irrecoverable. The filigree stairway that allowed the walls to dominate the ascent has been transformed into a solid base; above it the sheer surface of the walls is articulated by fine, barely perceptible horizontal rustication that moderates the severe, craggy space. The massive but carefully calibrated detail of steps, balustrade and handrail worked out in finely finished concrete makes the new stairway the proud focus of the whole building. Its breathtaking new vesture offers an eloquent tribute to Stüler's grandiose but spare proportions.

Above: Photograph of the gutted Staircase Hall, undated (presumed to be taken soon after the bombing on 23/24 November 1943).
Below: Photograph of the Historical Room with the Egyptian collection on the ground floor, undated.

Above: Photograph of the partially destroyed east wing of the Neues Museum, with the connecting bridge and the Altes Museum to the left, undated (after 3 February 1945).
Below: South façade of the Neues Museum with newly erected corner risalit and reconstructed south colonnade, 2009.

The reborn building now speaks anew to the visitor in accents that echo the intentions of its original designers and assumes the role of a witness to its own tragic story. Some have found this uncomfortable, while others have called for a 'total' restoration, which would only have been possible by glossing over the past. Yet others may prefer a museum neutered to a sterile museality.

For all that, the enthusiasm with which Berliners have crowded into the Neues Museum seems to show that its fresh guise may turn out to offer a testimony that will continue to be a more important *Mahnmal* than any specific or 'dedicated' monument. The fragmented history that it recounts through intricate overlays can speak to our time – and will, I suspect, speak to the future more clearly and sympathetically than did the grand pictorial narratives that it so convincingly presented to the visitors of an earlier age.

To have kept faith with Stüler's grand and spare proportions, to the inherent structure, has allowed Chipperfield to pay tribute to the harsh contradictions of the museum's history while reasserting its unity. That seems to me a great achievement.

The Art of Survival

Jonathan Keates

Wondrously ornate is the stone of this wall, shattered by fate;
The precincts of the city have crumbled, the ancient work of giants
Is fallen into decay.

These are the opening lines of *The Ruin*, an anonymous poem dated to the
10th century and surviving as part of a manuscript collection of Anglo-
Saxon verse in the library of a Cambridge college. It also happens to be the
earliest meditation in English on the sensory and imaginative impact created by a writer's encounter with a building. The poet is fascinated by the
moss-grown walls, the scarred tiles, 'the wide red roof of vaulted beams'
and the skill with which the architect, 'that bold-minded man', contrived to
bind the soaring columns together with hoops of iron.

As a lover of the tumbledown and the dilapidated, I understand how the
nameless Saxon bard must have felt. Nothing quite equals a ruin as an
image of human endeavour, a symbol of sheer obstinacy and persistence or
a vehicle for moralising, and it helps if the surroundings cohere. For the full
effect to work adequately, there has to be a suitable contrast set up between
ideas of somewhere and nowhere. The finest ruins of all, as a general rule,
stand in thick woodland, on the edge of deserts, concealed in olive groves,
or else spring up suddenly among featureless stretches of ploughland and
pasture. An essential quality of absence, created by elements such as
fallen statuary, shattered inscriptions or even something so simple as the
ruts made by ancient cartwheels in the stone threshold of a city gate, is
enhanced by the unpeopled nature of the landscape.

According to these criteria, Berlin's Neues Museum is hardly the most
promising of ruins. The city itself, as a physical entity, has always been
something of a paradox. 'How', wondered Stendhal, visiting in 1806, 'can
people erect a metropolis on sand so deep that your feet sink into it up to
the ankle?' Yet by the same token, the whole place, bombarded, divided and
now substantially reinvented, has become a metaphor of survival, its monumentality as inextinguishable as the mingled energies of its street life.
Permanent on top of its sandy impermanence, the somewhere shows no
signs of turning into a nowhere, as its refurbished buildings demonstrate,
even those which, like the Schloss, no longer exist except in the memory of
older inhabitants.

In this context there was a defiant quality, a sort of gruff, insouciant
shrug, about the Neues Museum when I first visited its blackened carapace
almost a decade ago. This was in February, when neither the weather nor
the light was calculated to offer a specially flattering introduction to the

Above: Ruin of the Neues Museum seen from north-west. Structural shell of Egyptian Courtyard in foreground (between 1970 and 1985).
Below: Central risalit with Staircase Hall while substitute foundations were being laid. The provisional stairs access the few rooms still in use on levels 2 and 3 of the east wing (between 1988 and 1994).

building, but this gloom managed somehow to enhance the air of sturdy autonomy clinging to Stüler's ravaged masterpiece. The presence of cement mixers and scaffolding wasn't necessarily a guarantee of continuity or work in progress. Given what was happening elsewhere in Berlin at that time, with every street, square, palace or *hinterhof* turned into a building site, these elements seemed just as much decorative as practical.

What, in any case, was to be the museum's ultimate destiny? The idea of it as hanging on, awaiting its hour, a creature of patient wisdom 'cased in the unfeeling armour of old Time',[1] had unquestionable appeal. Sooner or later the skirmishing would inevitably start as to how much of the surviving structure should be left to speak for itself and how cosmetic the process of restoration was intended to be. The most compelling image I retain of the building at this unresolved phase of its life is that of the great staircase hall without its stairs, forlorn beneath Stüler's soaring triple-light windows, their symbolism of enlightenment seemingly redundant.

No wonder David Chipperfield, proposing the Neues Museum's recovery, spoke of the 'dramaturgy' within this particular space. The word provides a key to the whole work as finally revealed to us. Drama is the most inalienably human of art forms, but the actors in this play have not been confined to the dedicated team which has overseen the project's passage to completion. There is a chorus formed by public opinion, by official voices from the state and the municipality, not to speak of professional experts, architectural journalists and critical onlookers. The scenario also embraces that element which playwrights and directors demand as essential to an authentic theatrical experience, the audience as involved participants, fully responsive to the ebb and flow of what is, as far as I can tell, a unique dramatic narrative.

Representative members of this cast have gathered in the vestibule of the completed Neues Museum. It is another chilly February day, 'the same, ten years later', as dramatists use to indicate as their setting for a final act. Never underestimate the continuing significance of time in a plot such as this one. Sadder and wiser by dint of experience than when we last appeared on this stage, we look for some kind of transfiguration or epiphany to redeem us. This is that kind of drama.

Almost at once the building's singular physicality gets to work. That 'in my end is my beginning' quality which seems to be part of the Museum's inherent wisdom, something surely intended by Stüler himself, appears in the way David Chipperfield has allowed sections of the fabric's brick core exposed by the trauma of bombardment and the subsequent ravages of the weather to play a significant role. A complete language of brick, enunciated by the different layerings, shades and surfaces laid bare for us by walls and vaulting, starts to resonate as part of that spectrum of damage presented to us elsewhere by shattered ceilings, chipped columns and cracked plaster.

The effect, we soon realise, is that of a palimpsest, a surface on which any number of texts have been written but only imperfectly erased, so that it

---

1 Line from the poem *Elegiac Stanzas, Suggested by a Picture of Peel Castle in a Storm, Painted by Sir George Beaumont* by William Wordsworth.

becomes possible for us to trace earlier fragments under existing lines. I'm reminded – and the link is scarcely accidental, given 19th-century Germany's absorption with classical antiquity – of those innumerable buildings in present-day Rome where masonry from the Middle Ages and the Renaissance has incorporated arches, columns or stretches of brickwork from temples and palaces dating from the time of the Caesars or even earlier. Italians sometimes call this *edilizia fagocitosa*, 'phagocyte building', because the visual impression is that of a digestive process in its initial phases, one structure, as it were, eating another and temporarily frozen in the act, so that the older material never wholly disappears. This is, if you like, the architectural equivalent of the ghost story, in which a 'presence' hangs over a particular locality so as to remind its residents or visitors that some promise or act of recompense has been left unfulfilled.

Fulfilment in the present case involves the Neues Museum being allowed by this means to tell its own story of hopes, expectations and assumptions over the course of 170 years. In the thrilling vista through the main exhibition halls, another of the overall drama's dominant episodes, we can see the synthesis of fragments and interpolations as a spirited dialogue, harmonious but carefully unresolved, a continuing pulse in the body of the museum. 'The form remains, the function never dies'.[2] This line from a favourite poem drums in my brain as we move from room to room, and it becomes ever clearer that David Chipperfield and his collaborator Julian Harrap have linked this kind of continuity to a deeper awareness of enduring line and volume within Stüler's building.

Such traces of the original décor that do survive are the more enthralling for their mercurial, fugitive quality, like the swatches of a couturier or the melodic jottings in a composer's notebook. I'm captivated by a sudden burst of blue on an Egyptian ceiling, a celestial cosmology complete with gilded hieroglyphs and a parade of constellations, evidence of the Prussian architect's belief that the exhibits on display should be presented to the viewer within a suitably sympathetic environment. As for the pillars and colonnades throughout the museum, these, more than any of the other architectural components, seem deliberately intended to elude our cravings for homogeneity in the visual language governing a decorative scheme. The museum is having none of such banality. There are great soot-blackened Grecian sequences, their Corinthian capitals and flutings chipped and abraded; there are Romanesque arcades conjured up from a memory of Italian church porticoes; doorways are flanked by elegant caryatids; and columns suggested by Philae or Luxor carry authenticating lotus patterns around their bulbous bases.

Most compelling for me of all such features is the frieze surrounding the *Griechischer Hof*, not least because of the pitiless abruptness with which the walls underneath the handful of plaster fragments still clinging to its lower edge fall away into the starkness of elemental brick,

2 Line from the poem *Afterthought* by William Wordsworth.

Above: The Staircase Hall after completion of the structural securing and provisional roofing in 1988–89, 2003.
Below: Staircase Hall with view of south wall and placement of supports in the restored western passageway, 2009.

with something almost menacing in the line of blind windows below. Both in style and theme, this set of high-relief sculptures by Heinrich Schievelbein is among the most flamboyantly 'period' items in the surface adornment of the museum. Its subject is *The Last Days of Pompeii*, the title of Edward Bulwer Lytton's late-Romantic historical novel, whose clever filtering of a modern *zeitgeist* through the prism of the classical past made it profoundly influential on readers throughout 19th-century Europe. The sculptured pageant serenely proposes that Pompeii should rise at last from centuries of entombment under layers of volcanic ash. Transcending the doom of history, it is to be reborn under the wise dispensation of Berlin's Neues Museum, where its artefacts will be exposed to view after eighteen hundred years of oblivion.

Schievelbein's Pompeiian frieze adorns a vast court to the south of the staircase hall. From the other side David Chipperfield's personal intervention as a living architect enters the discourse in the shape of a projecting platform beneath concrete posts and beams, with a glass roof above it. The surprise of this is total, both in the way it creates another zigzag in a continuously engrossing narrative and because it offers no obvious compromise with the decorative melange encountered elsewhere in the building. This is Chipperfield's signature on the Neues Museum, inscribed not as a gloss or footnote to the prevailing text, let alone as some arrogant graffito or 'tag' jostling for our attention, but as a carefully meditated independent episode, consistent in its simplicity with the idealism inspiring the original building. The platform's distinctive linearity, with a sudden intensification of light as we enter it, inducing a sense of bleached, heat-soaked walls, presents us with an atmospheric counterpart to Stüler's lotus columns and astronomical map of the heavens by evoking another Egyptian impression altogether to contextualise the pharaonic treasures on display.

I cling to this place as a moment of stasis among the rhythms and pulses of the building, like one of those crucial rests in a musical score where the spaces between each unit of sound become as audible as the notes themselves. Equally potent is Chipperfield's other addition to the museum, in the form of a tower at its south-eastern corner, an invention as different from the platform in character and associations as it's possible to imagine. Kiln, tomb chamber, oasthouse, beehive or dovecote? The structure arrests us initially by an intrinsic playfulness in its proportions, those of a brick rectangle which somehow resolves itself into a sinuous chimney soaring towards the cupola. Yet the unadorned immensity gathers within it a feeling of something far older than both the Neues Museum or indeed most of the archaeological riches contained here. Shapes as primal as this one, which seems to have been scooped out of its brickwork in one colossal tug of clenched fingers, return us to the Anglo-Saxon poet of *The Ruin* marvelling at 'the ancient work of giants'.

Just as the platform responds to already existing features in the building that have survived the damage done elsewhere, so the tower's curving hollow seems an inspired improvisation on another noteworthy structural theme in certain of the halls and galleries. This is Stüler's use of terracotta

Above: View from the Roman Room toward the North Dome Room, 2009.
Below: East wall of the Egyptian Courtyard with surviving original wall decoration
(Temple at Edfu + Isle of Philae), 2009.

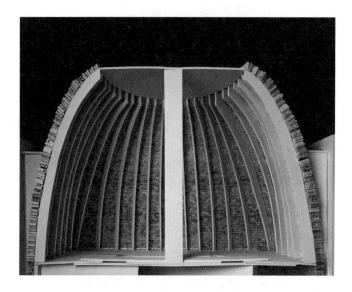

Above: North wall of the Greek Courtyard with the central motif from Hermann Schievelbein's plaster frieze *The Destruction of Pompeii*. In the centre Pluto sits atop Vesuvius and the winds are seen strewing lava rocks, 2009.
Below: Working model of the masonry for the new South Dome. In the course of execution planning, the model was used to work out details of the geometry and execution techniques. David Chipperfield Architects, 2003.

Above: The Egyptian Courtyard seen from gallery level, 2009.
Below: Working and presentation model for the reconstruction of the staircase used for preliminary planning, David Chipperfield Architects, 1999.

bowls and pots in the creation of the ceilings, so as to take the weight off the foundations, thereby challenging those who doubted that anything so grand as the Neues Museum could be raised on the treacherous sands of the surrounding island. Here and there a glimpse of the earthenware in these miniature domes transports us to that Mediterranean world for which German fantasy has pined since the days of Goethe's Mignon, with her longing for 'the land where the lemon trees bloom'. Surely some of the light irradiating the museum comes not from the inexorable clarity of a Berlin morning or from the high ideals and meticulous disciplines of Prussian scholarship, but from this simple hankering of the north for the south's promises of warmth and luminosity.

It's in the staircase hall that we grasp most effectively the truth that this building is more than the sum of its parts as the handsomest of vessels for a historic collection of antiquities. The welding of pre-cast concrete stairs to the beetling cliffs of brick at either side reinforces notions of survival and endurance, leaving the rule of light triumphant, 'restoring intellectual day' from those tall upper windows. The momentum within Chipperfield's concept of the staircase itself is as resistless as that created by the monumental flanking walls and those immense wooden roof trusses above them. The dramaturgy Chipperfield acknowledged in confronting the project is fully engaged and the rationale behind the broader enterprise of recovery and completion justifies itself most eloquently at this crowning instant.

The anonymous poet of *The Ruin* refers to the architect of the hall in the midst of the derelict city as 'that bold-minded man'. David Chipperfield's boldness has carried him further than a simple act of restoration, however comprehensive its reach. Responding to the eclecticism of the original designs, with their Etruscan-style ironwork, echoes of French Baroque landscape painting, evocations of the progress of German history or frescoed mythologies set within a Renaissance octagon, the modern architect has enlarged their combined perspective on the past to embrace another kind of inheritance altogether, Berlin's own momentous experience of the 20th century, in which the world's share has been universal. When I first saw the museum, I recall contrasting its prospect of apparently irredeemable bleakness, shadow and decay with the enthusiasm and conviction of Chipperfield and his team as they prepared to embark on the project. The redemption finally achieved, in which a new work is nurtured by an older one, constitutes an act of trust, not merely in the building and its creator but, perhaps more significantly, in humanity itself. That staircase hall is a challenge as much as a solution.

XVII

Contra-Amnesia: David Chipperfield's Neues Museum Berlin

Karsten Schubert

All of us are creatures of a day; the rememberer and the remembered alike.
Marcus Aurelius [1]

1

I visited the Museum Island for the first time in about 1978 with my mother.
To do so was still a Cold War adventure, involving a U-Bahn journey from
Zoo station in the West. On its way the train had to crawl through Kochstraße
station – closed since the day the wall went up – a pair of heavily armed
soldiers slowly pacing up and down its dimly lit platform. Stepping off the
train at Friedrichstraße station, we went through border control, had our
passports stamped, and exchanged West for East marks, which was com-
pulsory. Outside the station was a different world: dark, drizzly, damp,
drained of colour, with only a few streetlamps. A pall of brown-grey coal
smoke was hanging over everything and all sounds were muffled. There was
very little traffic and only a handful of pedestrians, who avoided eye contact
as they hurried into the fog. There was the odd bus, and from time to time
a Trabant car noisily spluttered past, its yellow headlights barely strong
enough to pierce the gloom. After a short walk we reached the Museum
Island, a blackened broken mass hardly discernible against the gloomy sky.
In order to get to the Pergamon Museum one had to cross a rickety steel
and wood bridge across the Spree River, the black water visible between
the planks. To the right was the Neues Museum, completely ruined and
without hope, behind it that ludicrous Gründerzeit wedding cake, the
Nationalgalerie. Inside the Pergamon Museum were hardly any other visitors, and my memory is very much of my mother and myself having the place
to ourselves. The interior felt particularly cold the way unheated buildings
do. The galleries were barely illuminated, with a strong smell of dust, floor
polish and stale canteen food hanging in the air. My strongest recollection
is not of the Pergamon Altar, the Milet Market Gate or the Ishtar monuments, but of the Spinario in a side gallery, self-absorbedly gazing at his
foot. Suddenly a train would rumble past the windows, disconcertingly high
and close, its lights momentarily swaying the forest of sculptures, and then
silence and darkness again. It was truly magical and still feels so thirty
years later.

After leaving the museums we tried, unsuccessfully, to spend our East
marks (as on your way out you had to hand back what you had not spent).

1 Maxwell Staniforth (translator), *Marcus Aurelius Meditations*, London: Penguin 1964, p. 72.

Above: Ruin of the Neues Museum with the walled-up former south entrance on Bodestraße,
photograph, undated.
Below: The Room of the Niobids on the main floor of the Neues Museum with the collection
of plaster casts of Hellenistic and Roman sculptures, view towards North Dome Room,
photograph, undated (before 1921).

To my surprise the shops really were empty; I had always thought that this was just counter-propaganda from our side. We finally found a bookshop where, alas, the only things on offer were Marx and Engels Collected Writings. I bought a set, not making much of a dent in our East Mark stash. We finally ended up at the Friedrichstraße station café, the interior blue with cigarette smoke, to have a cup of Ersatz coffee and some stale cake. We made quite an entrance. My mother was wearing a full-length black fur coat, which prompted stares from the clientele with a mix of idle curiosity and mild resentment. Whilst there was nothing wrong then with fur per se, it sure marked us as out as 'not from here'. Back at Friedrichstraße, we proceeded in reverse: through passport control, returning the leftover money and finally the five-minute journey back to the West. We stepped off the train at Zoo station – clutching Marx and Engels – and out into the dazzling brightness of the world we had left behind only a few hours ago.

2

In Berlin the ground is sodden with history, but unlike, say, in Rome, here it does not come with the comfort of distance or leisurely, mythologising (re-) telling. Here it is as if somebody had conducted a perverse experiment trying to figure out how much world drama could be crammed into the *smallest* amount of space in the *shortest* time *closest* to the present. Berlin, the Prussian capital, a backwater really, reborn as the capital of the first unified Germany and bloated by Gründerzeit industrialisation, two generations later re-imagined by Albert Speer as the capital of the world (to be renamed *Germania* after the war was won). A city bombed to smithereens, divided, each half turned autonomous in all its various functions, and finally made whole again. Not enough time has gone by to reconcile the past, and the various scars of destruction and repair are still purple and shiny. In some places it still looks as if the ground has been deep-ploughed with explosives, while in others a soothing calm has set in. The largest scar of all, the run of the wall, has healed surprisingly well, and it needs a trained eye to discern its serrated trajectory. The remnants of the Third Reich, on the other hand, are unavoidable, mostly because of their humongous scale. There are relatively few reminders of the GDR: proof, if really needed, that it is the victor who tells the story.

Like the city as a whole, the Neues Museum had been subjected to the hand of history's brutally accelerated ageing process. Its mid-19th-century architecture had been pummelled and eroded to a degree normally seen only in truly old buildings, resulting in material losses on a scale one associates more with antiquity. That this should have happened to a historicist structure only adds complexity and wonder to the result.

In the 1840s, Friedrich August Stüler designed the sequences of historicising interiors of the Neues Museum to provide backdrop and background information for the works of art on display. These suites were in turn introduced by Wilhelm von Kaulbach's mural cycle in the main staircase. The ensemble as a whole added up to a concise *weltbild*, if with a strong Germanic tilt, the grandest and final monument of Prussian Enlightenment.

Individual galleries were a deft and fanciful reinvention of particular chapters of the past, but each room was to be partly defaced, fragmented or completely erased by the ravages of war and subsequent weather exposure. Ironically, the rather over-the-top high-colour interiors of the 1850s never looked truer than today, as if the sole purpose of war and weather was to make them palatable to contemporary, more minimalist sensibilities. It is the best-preserved rooms, like the *Niobidensaal*, that seem gaudy and inauthentic.

The question of the Neues Museum's 'authentic state', much bandied about today, turns out to be a bit of a red herring. Begun in 1843 and structurally completed four years later, the final galleries and von Kaulbach's murals were not finished until a decade later. Within a few years, the process of gradual change and adaptation began, culminating with the installation of the new galleries for the Amarna finds in 1919/23. In a sense the building was never truly 'completed'. At the beginning of the Second World War the evacuation of the museum collections started the saga of their dispersal to East and West, many works never to be seen again, destroyed in their place of safekeeping, while others, for decades thought lost, reappeared in the Soviet Union, their ultimate fate still in the balance. Miraculously, most of the art was saved.

It was not only the politics and external historical circumstances that kept changing. The Neues Museum was an embarrassingly late child of the Enlightenment, the last attempt at a universal encyclopaedic museum organised under a single narrative arc, but by the time of its realisation the idea's moment had already passed. Universality had given way to specialisation, and the various components of the collection began to be considered autonomous. In collecting terms, the second half of the 19th century was a golden age, and as a result of an aggressive acquisition policy the Berliner Museen quickly began to burst at the seams. More and more of the specialist collections were then moved to other locations, in particular the Völkerkundemuseum, Schloss Monbijou and the Kunstgewerbemuseum (Martin Gropius Bau). With universality and 'completeness' no longer the primary goal, the plaster cast collection (which had taken up, after all, the entire central floor) disappeared from display. By the beginning of the 20th century the Neues Museum must have looked decidedly outdated, the galleries' decor speaking louder of the 1850s than the various periods they pertained to and their programmatic unity frayed. This may explain the accelerating pace of interventions to both the structure of the building and its thematic canon. To this day the museum's enduring influence can be sensed in every period interior setting in museums worldwide. Stüler's rather fanciful free-wheeling inventions have given way to a sober preference for actual period rooms, now painstakingly removed from their original settings and reassembled in museums.

Whatever damage was inflicted to the Neues Museum by changing curatorial fashion, it was minor compared to what happened during the Second World War. Repeated Allied bombings and finally the fierce battle for Berlin in 1945 left the building barely standing. While the Communist regime

Above: The Room of the Niobids after removal of the plaster cast collection, with the new exhibit of antique vases, view towards North Dome Room, photograph, undated (between 1921 and 1939).
Below: The Room of the Niobids after temporary post-war usage was discontinued, view towards South Dome Room, 2003.

Above: The Greek Courtyard following conversion to the 'Amarna Hall' in 1919–1923 by architect Wilhelm Wille, looking south, photograph, 1923/24.
Below: The Greek Courtyard following the bombing on 3 February 1945 that largely destroyed the 1920s installations, looking north, photograph, undated (presumed to be taken 1988/89).

patched the other structures on the Museum Island, the Neues Museum was left with minimal repair. This can partly be explained by its particularly ruinous state. More likely though, the neglect was the consequence of Stüler's thematic-didactic programme, which had become deeply problematic after 1945. Karl Friedrich Schinkel, at a pinch, could be re-interpreted as a forerunner of (socialist) modernism – his Altes Museum was clumsily restored – but Prussian historicism was, initially, a different matter. As the East Germans were not shy with bulldozer and dynamite, one can only assume that those in power must have had an inkling at least that, given enough time, Prussia and the GDR too could be moulded into a single, seamless narrative, something that indeed was beginning to happen in the 1980s (to great irritation in West Germany, where a claim on Prussia had also been filed). Reconstruction work on the Neues Museum finally began in earnest in the summer of 1989. A few months later the GDR had collapsed.

In the following decade a master plan was drawn up for the island, and the Bode Museum (2000–2006) and the Alte Nationalgalerie (1998–2001) were restored to great acclaim. The Neues Museum again remained the island's basket case. In 1993/94 and 1994–97, a complicated and lengthy competition for the revival of the Neues Museum was held. The restoration or repair of the Neues Museum represented a professional conundrum. With its convoluted history and precarious state of preservation, what were an architect's options? Not only was the building badly damaged, with forty percent of its substance gone, but central parts had been irretrievably destroyed – most importantly the main staircase and the west façade wing with the Egyptian Courtyard – the remainder smashed up and mangled beyond recognition. Many of the half-hearted rescue attempts had actually not alleviated but rather added to the problem. How exactly was one to put all these fragments back together, and make the delicate layering of history and Stüler's interior programme legible again while creating a building that could accommodate the demands of cultural tourism and meet today's rather stringent conservation and curatorial standards?

There were two conventional answers to this. One was to go for a faux authenticity, to conserve what was left and conjure up what was not and, depending on one's ethos, render the difference more or less unintelligible. The other approach was to introduce a new overriding architectural master narrative in order to unite the fragmentary remains and create a visual whole. Both options had their proponents, and the faithful reconstruction idea in particular had many vocal defenders. Both models stand in a long post-war tradition, one from time to time gaining general favour over the other, but ultimately neither was convincing enough to carry the day.

3

It was to the Neues Museum's benefit that neither model particularly fitted with the winning architect David Chipperfield's professional ethos. The thought of faking what was missing had already been ruled out by the client in the competition brief, and Chipperfield could not have agreed more. Not only would such a choice run against a modernist ethos, but too much of the building was missing to consider such a radical approach in all serious-ness. The building's historicism added a further complication. To recon-struct interiors that were a historicising fantasy raised the question of what exactly such a combination represented and how it might be perceived. The interiors would be inauthentic as to the period style they pertained to and inauthentic as to the period of their creation, doubly timeless in the worst Orwellian sense imaginable. The most pragmatic argument against a wholesale reconstruction was the observation that, as the building had such a drawn-out gestation period, there would have been difficulty agreeing on a terminus ante quem to which such reconstruction work might aspire, a specific point in time when the Neues Museum seemed to appear particularly finished or 'perfect'. As we have seen, until its war destruction, the museum was a place of evolving ideas, functions and uses, and such an 'ideal' moment was simply impossible to pinpoint because, as a matter of fact, it had never occurred. To restore towards a fictitious 'ideal' state would create a building that had never actually existed. How to indicate that the building had been in ruins for fifty-odd years posed an additional challenge.

Yet it was another consideration that was probably more decisive in the rejection of a 'faithful' reconstruction. If the museum – in its transition from a universal to a specialist enterprise – had come to put emphasis on the authenticity of displays *above all else*, and by extension had become the ultimate arbiter and guarantor of such authenticity, it was to follow that the same standard would also have to hold true about its container. Doubt about the authenticity of the container would, as if by osmosis, cast in doubt the authenticity of the content. Here the question of authenticity of setting, because of its proximity to content, became the central issue. It made a completely novel, unorthodox and delicate approach necessary.

Certain buildings are reconstructed faithfully for political and symbolic reasons; for instance, questions of authenticity were not central to the thinking behind the reconstruction of the Frauenkirche in Dresden. The building had become a potent stand-in for complete chapters of German history: Saxon past, the Second World War destruction of Dresden, post-war division and finally reunification. To rebuild the church was to signal national renewal and to attest to a past not forgotten but atoned. It was, above all, a declaration of faith in the future. Such clear-cut symbolism is rare. In Berlin, a few hundred metres from the Altes Museum, the planned Schloss reconstruction presents a different picture. If the symbolism of dynamiting the ruin in 1956 was obvious – the doing away with the key symbol of Prussian and German militarism – the thinking behind rebuilding the façade, re-naming the whole Humboldt Forum and then placing non-Western art museums inside, offers a catalogue of contradictory gestures: the bold, the apologetic and the politically correct negate one another, an anxiety-riven symbolic dog's dinner if there ever was one. The Neues Museum by the nature of what is, first and foremost, a museum, fortunately escaped the heavy hand of political symbolism. A place to regard the past, it was easier to adapt this perspective to regarding itself.

As for the question of a superimposed or unifying Chipperfield narrative, this idea was rejected too. Such an approach would have introduced a fourth storyline – aside from the historic building fragments, Stüler's iconographic programme, and the displays of art from Ancient Egypt and Pre- and Early History. A cacophony of voices would have been the result, or worse maybe, the historic fabric and displays could have been completely overwhelmed by the architect's intervention. Such an idea went against the architect's temperament too.

4

The answer to this catalogue of objections and considerations was as startlingly original as it was simple: Chipperfield would not approach this project like an architect but rather like a conductor, uniting a diverse chorus of expert voices, here teasing out a tender note and there suppressing a shrill outburst. Chipperfield's 'orchestra', despite its great diversity, roughly divided into two halves. On one side there were those who were primarily concerned with the historic fabric of the building. On the other side were the curators whose job it was to make a new home for their stellar collections and accommodate future armies of visitors and their myriad needs. Each fraction in turn had its own supporting cast, and back catalogues of well-rehearsed arguments. The trick was to give each side its say. The whole process could have easily deteriorated into an over-my-dead-body standoff, with both sides insisting on the primacy of their particular concerns over all else, and surely there must have been moments of nearly complete deadlock. Each sub-fraction – the architectural historians, the collection curators, the conservators, the museum pedagogues, the display designers, to name only a few – came with its own set of doctrinaire views and seemingly non-negotiable ground rules. Inevitably, new, unexpected coalitions formed and new rifts sprung up continuously, yet gradually and miraculously a workable consensus emerged. The Neues Museum was not a case of form following function, but rather a compromise to be reached between (historic) form and (contemporary) function. To achieve this delicate balancing act required countless cross-disciplinary meetings in which every aspect of the building and its purpose was discussed and the smallest detail considered in all its wide-ranging implications. It is here that a particular gift of David Chipperfield came in handy: his ability to synthesise contrary views and have everybody arrive, seemingly of their own volition, exactly where he needed them to be. The architect's hand is of course there, but it remained by and large invisible. The result is the stunning paradox of a building that is the architect's in essence and spirit but not in appearance.

I visited the Neues Museum for two days in June 2009. I had worried beforehand that the building's past would have either been wiped out in the reconstruction process, or worse, that some sort of ruin romanticism may have crept in. Another concern was that the building's strong character might get in the way of its function as a museum, that the displays might be overwhelmed by the drama of Stüler's ruin. I need not have worried. The museum had retained its particular qualities and all its scars, and if anything, the Stüler backdrop seemed to further enhance the function of the building as a home for the art of ancient Egypt and Pre-and Early History. My visit was scheduled just after the new display vitrines had arrived and been put in place. A casual remark somebody at Chipperfield's office had made a few weeks before, that the architect and his team had spent months thinking about the particular nature of the collections that will be on display, now made sense. It seemed like something that an architect should automatically do, but actually most recent museum buildings have gone up without such scrutiny or consideration. The results are museums that looked best empty, without art and visitors (and recent books on museum architecture show, without fail, empty buildings). Chipperfield's museum, on the other hand, felt as if something was missing when empty, and with the vitrines in place it became clear why this should be the case: the place was thought out with the displays in mind. No doubt when full of visitors it will look even better.

As for the restoration work, its rhythm and tone seem to change gently from room to room, depending on states of preservation and the character of Stüler's inventions. Entirely rebuilt rooms follow Stüler's outlines and echo – in material and colour – the rest of the building. Restored spaces range from the highly fragmentary to the fully preserved. The result is an enfilade of galleries of varying textures and densities. Often the displays and interiors are in dialogue. For instance, there is the rather catacomb-like basement space housing granite and marble sarcophagi; a large new stone-walled gallery houses the three Berlin mastabas, their monumentality subtly echoed by the architecture of the space; the Amarna Courtyard will display a group of the famous plasters and sandstone trial pieces found in Thutmose's studio. The most spectacular setting, the rotunda, its dome loosely based on the Pantheon in Rome, will contain the bust of Nefertiti. Her own rather gaudy colour and the high colour of the walls are in mutually beneficial dialogue. In the *Moderner Saal* the flow is suddenly interrupted by the appearance of a cast of Lorenzo Ghiberti's Gates of Heaven for the Baptistry of St John's in Florence, a reminder of what the first-floor gallery originally contained: the comprehensive collection of plaster casts. Fractured high drama in one gallery gives way to serenity and classicist restraint in the next, followed again by visual theatre – a succession of subtly graded surfaces and changing tones.

The changing rhythms of the spaces are not just a matter of aesthetics but also serve an important pedagogic function: they are a constant reminder to the visitor of the particular power of the museum as an ordering device. Instead of lulling him into a stupor with a succession of virtually identical spaces in which displayed objects appear as if there naturally, the changes of mood, emphasis and style keep him alert to the museum's interpretative and normative power and the ideology-driven selectiveness of displays. Stüler's fragmentary narrative programme is a welcome reminder that such storylines are not objective and writ in stone but can date and lose validity with changing times and circumstances, making today's history (with its claim to impartiality and objectiveness) tomorrow's historicism.

Chipperfield's Neues Museum, with its layering of both the past and the contemporary, makes the visitor aware that history is not static but always, first of all, a reinterpretation through contemporary eyes, driven and inflected by current agendas. The works of art on display, Stüler's programme and the traces of destruction and reconstruction are a constant reminder of this, bringing the past closer and making the visitor an active participant in its constitution. Here history has not been stilled but stays tantalisingly alive.

Museum as Palimpsest

Kenneth Frampton

As we enter the end of the first decade of the 21st century, it would be hard to find any other work in Germany which is as redolent with the entire trajectory of German history as the recently restored Neues Museum in Berlin, from the resurgence of a German national identity following the defeat of Napoleon in 1815, to its destruction at the end of the Second World War, and the long hiatus of the Cold War that in East Germany meant that certain kinds of reconstruction were barely feasible. A vast historical lapse separates the restored Neues Museum, opened to the public in October 2009, from the first architectural efforts to transform Berlin into the cultural and political capital of the emergent Prussian state, prominent among these being Karl Friedrich Schinkel's Altes Museum, realised in the *Lustgarten* over the years 1824–1830. This was followed in 1841 – the year of Schinkel's death – by Frederick William IV's romantic sketch of the Museum Island, conceived as an improbable 'sanctuary for art and science'. This sketch, influenced by Schinkel's designs for a royal palace on the Athenian Acropolis, was to be fleshed out by a succession of grand museums, beginning with Friedrich August Stüler's Neues Museum, completed in 1859, and going on to include Johann Heinrich Strack's (Alte) Nationalgalerie (1867–1876) and Alfred Messel's neo-classical Pergamon Museum, finally completed in 1930 by Ludwig Hoffmann. Of all these, the only museum to be conceived as a literal complement to the Altes Museum was the Neues Museum which, as Bernhard Maaz has pointed out, was conceived according to the Hegelian division of world history into the mythical, classical and romantic ages. That Stüler was Schinkel's prime pupil, inheriting the mantle, so to speak, at the time of the master's death, is borne out by the façade of the Neues Museum, which in so many respects is an essay in Schinkelesque Neoclassicism, with the exception of the pavilionated domes at either end of its eastern front. Where Stüler departed categorically from Schinkel was in the plan, which, aside from the systematic structure of the galleries, was more empirical and episodic in character. This last had the advantage of allowing it to function as a didactic museum of universal scope. As Maaz has written, citing the research of Hartmut Dorgerloh:

> [...] the Neues Museum was committed to an ideal and idealistic notion of completeness and was designed to reflect a theoretical idealised image of history as an 'instructive historical narrative'. Art and history were meant to elucidate and explain each other. The existing collections were meant to be supplemented and elucidated by gypsoplast reproductions and by wall paintings of historical events. Art could be experienced

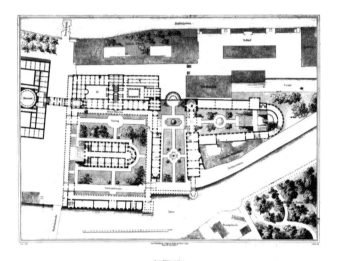

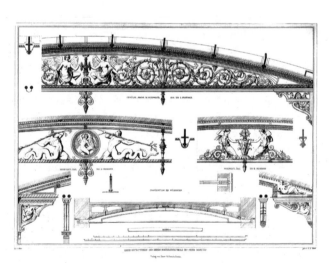

Above: Friedrich August Stüler's ideal plan for Museum Island, site plan.
Lithograph from: F.A. Stüler, *Das Neue Museum in Berlin*, Ernst & Korn, Berlin, 1862, plate 2.
Below: Detail drawings of the iron construction elements in the north wing.
Lithograph from: F.A. Stüler, *Das Neue Museum in Berlin*, Ernst & Korn, Berlin 1862, plate 8.

by documenting past periods of world history, as something that needed to be explained, and the wall paintings could be used to explain many testimonies to the history of mankind. The fact that this decorative scheme appeared plausible only in the context of its time and during the first few years following the opening of the museum, did not deter the designer from decorating the rooms in this way. [...] The wall paintings in these eighteen rooms formed a number of cycles in historic topography, mythology, and religion as well as historic subjects. They were preserved as the educational backdrop to the objects and now represent unique testimonies to the high ideals of their time regarding education and completeness.[1]

Stüler was heir to the *Schinkelschüler* tradition in other respects, in that he inherited his master's penchant for integrating new technology with traditional form and, as a result, participated in the debate as to the various ways in which heavy and light forms of construction could be significantly combined to create a new tectonic whole, to which the exposed, bowstring cast- and wrought-iron trusses of the Neues Museum bear witness. As Werner Lorenz remarks, Stüler not only conceived of uniquely hybrid tectonic forms, combining lightweight metal components with stereotomic masonry, but also pioneered the early use of rail tracks, steam locomotion and tower cranes to facilitate the efficiency and speed of erection.[2]

The cultural goals and aspirations incorporated in Stüler's original design remind us how such technical advances would, in one form or another, run throughout the history of the building from its very inception to the cultural complexities encountered in the processes of both its initial realisation and its current restoration. Prominent in this regard was the fact that the unstable marshy soil of the Museum Island was such that the buildings had to be erected on the top of timber piles, a foundation technique that, with the eventual rotting of the timber, would be recovered in the restoration process by driving 2,500 steel-clad concrete piles into the old foundations, reaching down to load-bearing layers some 32 m below the ground. It was this endemic instability that encouraged Stüler to lighten his original structure as much as possible through the use of iron elements such as had been pioneered in England and France – by Joseph Paxton in the Crystal Palace of 1851 and by Henri Labrouste in the Bibliothèque Ste Geneviève, also completed in 1851. In one way or another all of this was part of the legacy that David Chipperfield and his restoration architect Julian Harrap had to confront when they finally tackled the task of rebuilding the ruin.

The Neues Museum is still, and in some sense always was, a kind of palimpsest in which the past and the present mutually reflect one another at different scales through an unending series of ricochets, which include,

1 Bernhard Maaz, 'Architecture – Décor – History of Ideas', in: *The Neues Museum Berlin*, Leipzig: Seemann Verlag 2009, p. 28.
2 Werner Lorenz, 'Core Form and Artistic Form – The Art of Construction in Prussia Under the Influence of Industrialisation', in: *The Neues Museum Berlin*, Leipzig: Seemann Verlag 2009, p. 38.

among other conjunctions, the exhibition of 3,500-year-old Egyptian relics against a backdrop of Stüler's didactic scenography. The vicissitudes of similarly shifting temporal moments are also evident in Chipperfield and Harrap's restorative protocol wherein, assisted by peerless German technicians, they would piece together the torn tapestry of Stüler's period rooms. This subtle, continuously fractured, *mise en scène* would occasionally give way in the process of restoration to revealingly ingenious modes of construction, as in the reconstruction of the hollow pot, shallow-domed vaults that Stüler borrowed from John Soane's Bank of England. This mode of fabrication was painstakingly replicated once the design team had found a manufacturer who was able to produce clay pots of the kind that Soane had used, whereupon they proceeded to order 40,000 such pots for the purpose of rebuilding the domes. This was a modest number compared to the 1,350,000 used bricks that the team had to scavenge here and there throughout Europe, including 500,000 bricks from a single abandoned Prussian barracks in Silesia. Elsewhere, as in the walls of the main stair hall, where the brick had long since been stripped of its plaster, burnt during the war and subsequently exposed to the weather, the embrittled surface was merely cleaned, repaired, and re-pointed. Chipperfield's sensitive handling of this central space was the one feature in the consultant phase of the competition that gave him the edge over Frank O. Gehry's rival design, which featured extravagant spiral staircases transforming the former honorific volume of the stair hall into a gyrating vortex. It says everything about Chipperfield's respect for the potential layering of the past that he had originally conceived of relieving the bareness of the brick stair hall with the original cartoons of Wilhelm von Kaulbach's six-part didactic mural representing the history of mankind, which was totally destroyed during the war.

War and the combined destructive forces of nature and man are everywhere in evidence in this reconstructed museum, so that there is barely a single room where one is not constantly reminded of the way in which the transformations of time have impacted the fabric at every conceivable level, square centimetre by square centimetre, as one proceeds step by step through the itinerary. In all of this meticulous restoration, the architects have followed the recommendations of the 1964 International Charter for the Conservation and Restoration of Monuments – known as the 'Venice Charter' – which endorsed the time-honoured Ruskinian principal that, as far as possible, one should always retain the depredations of time and forego any attempt at a facsimile. The Chipperfield team adhered to this precept, even to the extent of preserving the trace of the redecorated rooms of the mid-1920s, when the curatorial elite of the moment modified Stüler's picturesque scenography in order to bring the galleries into line with the modern taste of the epoch. Otherwise, the general stratagem was to oscillate continually between the reparation of the old and the abstraction of the new, thereby augmenting the remains of the original stucco-work with new plaster, laid flush with its surface, or, alternatively, applying a tinted slurry to the adjoining brickwork in order to homogenise the overall tone and colour of a particular sequence. When there was no choice but to rebuild large

Above: Reconstruction of clay pot vault using original techniques, ceiling of the Ethnographical Room, 2004.
Below: Hedwig Schultz Völcker, Perspectival rendering of the Staircase Hall with exhibits from the plaster cast collection, watercolour, ca. 1910.

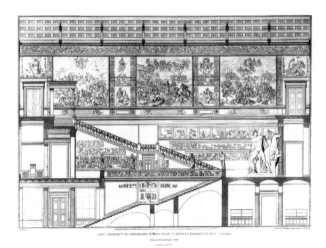

Above: Longitudinal section of the Staircase Hall with murals by Wilhelm von Kaulbach. Lithograph from: F.A. Stüler, *Das Neue Museum in Berlin*, Ernst & Korn, Berlin 1862, plate 17. Below: Sketch by David Chipperfield for the placement of columns and roof construction of the new Egyptian Courtyard, 1999.

segments of the original structure from scratch, Chipperfield used fair-faced brickwork, inside and out, made up of used bricks in the case of the destroyed north-west quadrant and the south-eastern dome, this last being reconstructed within as a tectonic, corbelled volume of a quasi-Roman-cum Assyrian character. The largely rebuilt, top-lit Egyptian and Greek court-yards are covered with new, lightweight ferro-vitreous roofs in order to assist in the stabilisation of the overall structure. These roofs are differently supported in each instance by Chipperfield's 'standard' 50 × 50-cm reinforced concrete piers.

The anachronistic 19th-century rendering technique known as marble cement would play a salient role in the reconstitution of this work at different levels. It would be employed in its most refined form in the reparation of marble mouldings and in the delicate reconstruction of the fluting of fractured classical columns. The basic material of this technique, related to stucco-lustro, is a high-fired, gypseous alabaster imported from Volterra in Italy. Mixed with marble dust, it is employed in this instance to simulate Carrara marble. One of the most challenging aspects of resorting to this gypsum technique, particularly when used for restoring delicate architec-tural detail, is that it takes four hours to set up and that, during this time, the crafted profile has to be maintained by frequent re-shaping. Such virtually lost techniques and methods appear at unexpected junctures throughout this restoration, including the complex techniques used to repair Stüler's wire-reinforced plaster ceilings, which he had been one of the first to pio-neer in Germany.

From a strictly architectural standpoint, the most expressive moments necessarily come to the fore in Chipperfield's totally new interventions, made of precision-cast reinforced concrete with a mix comprising white cement, local sand and marble aggregate. This material makes for a strik-ingly luminous white appearance in the larger primary volumes, such as the ten-pier hypostyle hall of the Egyptian Courtyard or the massive body of the main stair rising through three floors. In both instances we are presented with strictly abstract forms where Chipperfield handles everything as a 'zero-degree' statement, so as to foreclose the least possibility of kitsch somehow entering into the rebuilt fabric. While this may well accord with the rigorous standards of the Venice Charter, the total absence of detail tends to leave one deprived of any transitional junction or edge. One feels this particularly strongly in the minimalist, glass balustrading to the mezza-nine in the Egyptian Hall, in which, 50 × 50-cm, 15-m-high concrete piers slide past the translucent balustrade without a trace, as it were. This ten-dency to avoid the articulation of potential joints or seams is in contrast to the interstructural balustrading on the floor below, not to mention the artic-ulate jointing of metal and glass in the display cases designed by Michele de Lucchi. Chipperfield's seamless syntax obtrudes even more forcibly in the main stair, whereby the moulded handrails, cast in concrete, are more visible as shadow lines from above than from below, thus heightening one's awareness of the abstract character of the stair. Such austerity, heightened by the absence of Kaulbach's murals, emphasises that other absence which

Stüler provided but which Chipperfield and his client have been reluctant to simulate, namely, the crowning portico at the top of the stair: Stüler's caryatid porch based on the ancient Erechtheion, as a symbolic, humanist goal in a progressive history of mankind. This antique absence returns us in retrospect to the axial stairway and belvedere in Schinkel's Altes Museum which looked out upon a panorama of an emergent Berlin, a prospect featuring the Bauakademie and the Friedrichswerdersche Kirche. Stüler seems to have responded to Schinkel's extroverted didactic space with his own introverted rhetoric, namely, an equally axial stair hall which, since it hypothetically represented the progress of humanity, had to have a comparable optical focus, however theatrical this might be. This surely must, to some extent, account for Stüler's adoption of a pavilionated form similar to the caryatid screen in the Roman Baths at Sanssouci. Given that the armature of Stüler's portico, stripped of its sensuous form, was still in place at the time of the museum's utmost dereliction, one cannot help speculating as to the argument Chipperfield must have had with himself and with the client body in finally deciding not to evoke this missing iconic element. It is instructive to note that as late as 2003, Chipperfield still envisaged mounting a six-column portico at the head of the stairs which at one point, with its cylindrical columns, was almost a neo-classical trope. In a model of the reconstructed stair hall made shortly afterward, the portico assumed the character of an orthogonal matrix, vaguely reminiscent of the work of Sol LeWitt. This would not only have been consistent with the abstract syntax of Chipperfield's other interventions, but it would also have turned the cycle of history back upon itself in as much as such a form would have resembled the equally abstract composition of Friedrich Gilly's *Pfeilerhalle* of 1796, which ironically enough, given the present context, was a project for a mausoleum. As it is, we cannot entirely dispel the aura of a requiem that emanates from the restored *Treppenhalle*. It is indelibly there in the seared brick walls and the heavy, dark oak trusses hovering uneasily above. It is an atmosphere that recalls Anselm Kiefer at his most elegiac, this condensation of a catastrophic chain of events that can never be entirely redeemed by any restoration, no matter how brilliantly discreet its method and form.

If we may conflate, as one may in English, the word 'story' with the word 'history', then there are at least seven stories that are inextricably woven together in the renovation of this old/new museum, enough narratives we may say for any muse, even if we do not count the panoply of legends painted and inscribed onto and into the walls of building. For a start, there is the origin of the institution itself along with its mythical island. Then there is the epic story extending from the opening of the museum in the middle of the 19th century to its destruction 88 years later, a trajectory intimately linked to the history of a traumatised Germany divided and belatedly reunited. Finally, there is the more recent, regrettable story of the first competition of 1993/1994, won by Giorgio Grassi with a scheme that was subsequently rejected by the client. More recently still there is the saga of the building's reconstruction, block by numbered block, the impossible peristylar jigsaw laid in place tonne by tonne along the eastern front of

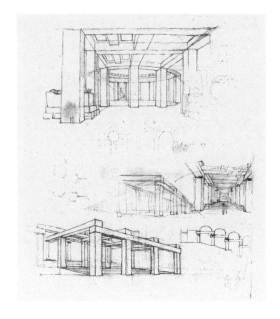

Above: Photograph of the Erechtheion Hall at the top of the staircase, undated.
Below: Friedrich Gilly, *Pfeilerhalle*, graphite and red ink, 40.6 × 34.2 cm, lost, formerly at the Royal Technical College of Charlottenburg, Berlin.

the building. In the last analysis it is this penultimate story of its painstaking rebirth that turns the building into an astonishing amalgam of high- and low-tech restorative methods – the freezing of ground, the application of carbon steel in the reinforcement of old iron, the ingenious insertion of all manner of sophisticated environmental services, cunningly hidden from the eye, transforming the entire achievement into a demonstration of the empirical prowess of late modern technology and science. A tour de force by any standards, and an enigmatic poem in itself, one that, given the unique combination of resources and skill, could perhaps have only been achieved in Germany, at this particular moment in history, to the designs of two discretely sensitive and resilient British architects.

XXVII

XXIX

Freezing the Ruin

Julian Harrap

It has been said that the treatment of the external wall surfaces of the
Neues Museum represents a decision to freeze time at the point of intervention. It allows the ruinous aspect of the building to be presented while at the
same time ending the process of decay and thus the life of the building as a
ruin. Some will argue that the consolidation of the crumbling wall surfaces
in this state is a form of dishonesty. The fragile fabric is now held in an
artificial state of suspension, denied its natural course of continual decay
and its eventual and inevitable loss. However, this approach manages to sit
coherently within the framework of the repair philosophy established for
the Neues Museum as a whole, which heightens its credibility as a solution.
It emphasises the essential design parameters, which have applied throughout the whole of the conservation process.

We might be deterred from enjoying ruins by those who have enjoyed
them in the past. To the 18th and 19th-century visitor the Coliseum was not a
ruin but a Monument commemorating the Roman Empire. Rulers' ambitions
are attracted by the endurance of masonry whereas the lover of ruins is
attracted by their sense of transience and vulnerability. The Architect is frequently at odds with the Archaeologist. To one the ruin may be manipulated
as any artefact can be for visual effect, while to the other every fragment is
a part of a jigsaw or a puzzle to which there is only one correct answer.

When Schinkel and Stüler came to London to visit Sir John Soane at his
museum and to travel north to see the mills of Lancashire, they were shown
the lightweight clay pot construction at the Bank of England. They would
have also seen Joseph Michael Gandy's visionary painting of the Bank
buildings as a grand monumental ruin. How strange it is to see Stüler's
great 19th-century Neues Museum wrecked and ruined as Piranesi or Gandy
might have illustrated. What an inspirational vision, redolent with history,
culture and the tragedy of ruination. How fortunate it is, in retrospect, that
the natural wish to expunge the injuries of war was delayed by political
division and lack of funds.

In a recent account of the current work on the Neues Museum, the architectural critic Hugh Pearman stated, 'I can guarantee that you have never
seen architecture quite like this before'. The need to invent a special architectural language to suit the particular circumstances of the Neues Museum
was immediately recognised by the Architects when their proposals were
submitted in 1997. The standing edifice has been described as a ruin imbued
with all the picturesque romanticism of 19th-century Arcadia. However, it
was more complex than that. It was a ruin that had survived since wartime,
but which had been tortured by a utilitarian and brutal consolidation under-

Above: Ruin of the Neues Museum with view of severely damaged central risalit housing the main staircase (between 1970 and 1985).
Below: The ruined west wing of the Neues Museum with makeshift roof. As the ceilings have been destroyed, the view from the Renaissance Room extends through all storeys, 1993.

taken since the Second World War. Elements of the romantic ruin remained, and were redeemable, but great swathes of what survived after the war had been swept away and the remainder cruelly corseted in concrete and steel with unsympathetic red engineering brick.

The challenge was to invent a new architecture which would bring back the wholeness of the building that would see both additions and subtractions to the existing structure. The old parts of the building needed to be, in a sense, cleansed of their corrupting consolidation, to provide a new value to the surviving fabric from the mid-19th century, while the new additions were to provide a re-establishment of the 19th-century spatial sequence of galleries around two private courtyards. This resulted in a small new addition to the building in the south-east corner and a three-storey over-basement L-shaped structure redefining the north-west corner of the former Egyptian Courtyard.

Following the devastation of the Second World War there was a natural desire for the building to rise from the ashes, and to overcome the past by expunging the pain of conflict. This is the natural political and emotional reaction to war and natural disaster. It is exemplified and served by the comfort offered by the Beaux Arts tradition of restoration. The alternative philosophy evolved by the Neues Museum team was to clarify and retain the evidence of the damaged building. The building was to be preserved with the evidence of its ruination, while sensitively creating a new architecture to make good those areas that had been lost. Three documents were prepared to guide the process of repairing the existing structure – The Conservation Guidelines, Concepts, and Strategy. These were specially written and developed, rather than resorting to the generalities of the accepted texts based on the Venice and Burra charters. They provided detailed studies of all the elements of structure, walls and ceiling surfaces on a room-by-room basis, and provided a framework for the design of the new building. The result was an over-arching methodology that sought to establish a sound intellectual basis against which the new design and the conservation work might be judged. They laid down the level of repair and intervention to the existing fabric that was to be tolerated.

It was deemed necessary to ensure a united composition within which the pre-existing ruin could be read and studied closely without deception or loss of confidence in the reality of what survives. The north-west wing was entirely rebuilt with an external envelope of salvaged brickwork, whose colour was selected and developed to bring a cohesive tonal and textural relationship to the adjacent surviving elements of sub-brickwork and render. The fenestration pattern mirrors that of the original façade, and the design was pared down to the essential skeletal essence of solid and void. The striation of the elevation with horizontal courses of projecting brickwork provides a reference to the rustication of the existing neo-classical elevation.

The surface treatment of the exterior of the building was conceived as being identical to the strategy for the interior. A certain level of cleaning, replacement and repair of the existing fabric was necessary, including the removal of previous unsympathetic repairs. Missing and damaged areas of classical detail were assessed individually, and a minimum amount of stonework was introduced to provide physical and conservational support to the surviving material. Each case was judged on its merits, with the view that the existing material must always be seen to take priority. The evidence of shrapnel attack has consciously been left as part of the building's history. The intention was to never deceive the viewer. The new stone was rarely manipulated to suit its juxtaposition with the old, and will be left to develop a patina of age over the coming decades. The impatience of the Berliners to see the building repaired is understandable, but it may be several decades before the design intentions of the restoration are fully understood.

Some aspects of the approach to the Neues Museum are unique, but many will point to the work of Hans Döllgast for the repair of the Alte Pinakothek, another war-damaged museum, originally constructed in 1836. His approach here was to re-establish the skeletal form of the exterior of the building, leaving the skin – including the window dressings and render – roughly torn away by the disaster of war. This was combined with a completely radical reordering of the interior which introduced two spectacular ramped staircases providing access to the three floors of neo-classical galleries. In its conception it is brilliant, but the architectural language is far simpler, and less complex and sophisticated, than the demands laid on the Berlin team by the surviving elements of the Neues Museum.

Internally, every room in the Neues Museum was treated differently according to its design and decoration when first built in the mid-19th century, as well as in accord with its surviving condition after war damage. The extraordinarily different levels of the survival of interiors were a profoundly significant factor in the making of decisions about the degree of conservation and repair. Some interiors had only faint remnants of their original decorative scheme, while others appeared, superficially, to be almost complete. The architectural programme for the original building was remarkably innovative. The Neues Museum was the first three-storey museum in Europe, with the great stair hall acting as an interior landscape space from which the galleries were entered at ground, first and second-floor levels. The treatment of the internal gallery wall surfaces has been the subject of much deliberation. The internal walls were treated in order to preserve the evidence of the plight of the interiors, while maintaining, and in some cases reinforcing, the language of 19th-century detailing. What remained is shown in its original colour and finish, provided with a supporting contextual surface of toned brickwork, render or plaster, which was moderated in a textural way to suit the various circumstances. New second-hand brickwork infills have been pointed to distinctly differentiate the levels according to their context. For example, old and decayed brickwork cannot reasonably be juxtaposed with flush pointing. The new work must have its pointing recessed in order to emphasise the colour of the brick and not the pointing. To convey this to the conservators and workers on site demanded an exceptional number of detailed drawings and a high level of site supervision by the conservation team.

Besides the brick, stone and iron of the building's construction, there are large areas of surviving painted decoration which required contextualisation. Originally these wall paintings had served a didactic purpose in providing an informing context for the exhibits within the galleries. With the new programme of display, this will no longer be the case, but nevertheless, the contribution of the decorative work forms such a substantial part of the surviving building that its visual importance had to be recognised. The technical processes of securing, cleaning and protecting the figurative and architectural paintwork is a subject beyond the scope of this essay. However, the methodologies are internationally established, although the resulting outcomes differ surprisingly in quality. The conservation design issue was to provide a suitable framework, often referred to as a 'picture frame', around the areas of randomly generated damage to enable the eye as far as possible to conjecturally complete the image or architectural pattern. Soane adopts this same technique in 1824. The level at which this was introduced had to be assessed on an individual wall or plane basis. It was made more problematic because of the inevitable and irrepressible desire of the conservators to clean the original surviving material to a pristine state. At the concept stage, the dusty antique quality of some of the images made them far easier to deal with than when they were somewhat over-cleaned and presented to the design team. This led to the necessity to review and reinforce the level of supporting interventions to provide the essential context for the surviving elements. In many instances we would have wished to cool the clean images with tone but this was prohibited.

The critical issue in taking surviving wall paintings, decorative architectural paintings or figurative work was the need to avoid commemorating the line of damage defining the edge of the surviving surface. This edge becomes extraordinarily bold and corrupts the architectural language of the interior in a powerful way. One only has to look at the results achieved in the *Römischer Saal* to understand how alarming this can be. This architectural interior may be compared with many others throughout the museum, such as the *Niobidensaal* and the *Roter Saal*, where damage of a similar order has been addressed in a very much more articulated manner. It is remarkable that the very clear Guidelines, Strategies and Concepts for the interiors have led to such wide and divergent interpretation. Perhaps these issues will receive further consideration in the future when the museum is dressed with exhibits.

The conservation of the floor surfaces could perhaps be construed as something of a compromise. In an ideal world, the conservation of the floor plates from which the arcaded interiors of the galleries rise should have been undertaken on the same basis as the wall and ceiling planes. However, such are the numbers of visitors that the museum will receive, that the conservative techniques of injecting voids between the substrate layers of the under-render to consolidate them was restricted because of the density of traffic to which they would be subjected. All the conventional exploratory research was undertaken, including the sourcing of the stone and terracotta and encaustic tiling, to enable conservative renewal to be undertaken. In anticipation of around 1 million visitors per year, a level of repairs had to be undertaken that was rather more rigorous than the ideal. The alternative would have been to protect the floors with carpeted walkways or even with suspended, glazed platforms such as those adopted over the ancient mediaeval floors of cathedrals or archaeological sites.

The central staircase hall is a striking space reaching the full height of the building's three floors. It is central to the visitor's experience of the museum. Sections of the wall were rebuilt with alternate bands of striated industrial red brick and edge-laid terracotta blocks to provide a ventilated cavity behind the Kaulbach frescos, which have been entirely lost. This involved removing large areas of engineering brick that had been introduced as part of the consolidation works carried out in the 1980s. Some have argued that this removal was inconsistent with the overall philosophy of the scheme, as interventions done under the GDR should have been retained as part of the history of the building. This is to misunderstand the difference between an archaeological and an architectural approach. The architects felt justified in returning to a recreated state of ruination as recorded in photographs at the point before the 1980s interventions. This was the basis of considerable debate, but the authorities were eventually convinced that this was a necessary measure in restoring a sense of harmony to the disjointed museum structure. Second-hand bricks and hand-made terracotta blocks were carefully chosen to match the existing sections of wall. The newly built areas have been delineated in such a way that it is still possible to tell, on careful inspection, what has been rebuilt. The limited remaining plaster has been successfully secured and areas of smoke blackening caused by the fire following the bombing have been retained. Continuity between old and new surfaces has been achieved through an intellectual programme of repair and consolidation that manages not to stifle the evidence of the ruin and allows the building's history to continue to emanate from its walls.

The new stair is a massive and monumental structure executed in high-quality pre-cast marble concrete with carefully chosen stone aggregates. The elements of the stair that are to be touched, such as the treads and handrails, are polished, while the rest of the structure has been distressed to provide a roughened finish. This interesting sensory contrast is both tactile and visual. Stüler's vision of the staircase was as garden architecture, achieving a sense of transition where one is neither outside nor inside the museum proper.

Striding across the western elevation of the stair hall is a colonnaded bridge which links the circulation route between galleries at the second-floor level. This is constructed of reclaimed coffered brickwork supported on massive fluted marble columns. For decades the columns had lain on their sides in an exposed outside location, leaving visible watermarks running horizontally across the shafts. After an articulate and closely argued debate, it was decided to leave this evidence of weathering visible to subtly explain the columns' history to the visitor.

The upper level of the Stüler staircase was crowned with an interpretation of the Erechtheion as marking the entrance to the curtilage of the Athenian Acropolis. This served both as a crowning monument to the stair

Above: The Renaissance Room after restoration. The columns were restored using the broken shafts supplemented with new drums.
Below: West façade of the Neues Museum. Detail of the main storey with conserved historic render, local render repair and exposed brickwork, harmonised with a toned slurry, 2008.

and also as an entry point to the smaller galleries on the second-floor level. Much debate arose around the possibility of the reintroduction of a similar feature that would provide this sense of threshold, but it was ultimately concluded that an architectural language was not available to fulfil this purpose.

Stüler's use of radical constructional techniques, informed by his visits to England, was not simply a reflection of advances in building technology, but was also constrained by the need to build, as lightly as possible, on brick walls supported on timber piles sunk into the river sand. Many devices were used to reduce the weight of the floors, including terracotta pot domes and vaults as well as porous lightweight bricks for walls on the upper floors.

The new rooms of the north-west wing have been defined by new walls on the line of the original. There has been a conscious decision to build in a monumental fashion. The new rooms are sometimes described as 'neutral' spaces, but most visitors will see them as chambers of great personality, style and elegance. This is emphasised by the use of high-quality, finely detailed marble concrete. Black-framed cases and lighting will complete the effect.

In contrast to the removal of the red stabilisation brickwork, some parts of the museum's later history have been retained and celebrated. The arrival of the Amarna collection in 1923 led to a series of alterations, some of which have been reinstated. One example is the newly constructed entrance within the vestibule at ground-floor level, where a draught lobby, dressed in dark brown leather studded with bronze buttons, provides a setting for the original 19th-century walnut and embossed bronze doors. Such a sumptuous entrance prepares the visitor for the majestic ascending stair and the elaborately decorated galleries leading off to the north and south. To the north is the *Mythologischer Saal* with its cobalt blue hieroglyph ceiling, while to the south is the *Vaterländischer Saal* with a magnificent frieze of Nordic images above pastel blue walls.

The principal galleries are side lit from the exterior elevations of the building and the majority are entered on axis between pairs of bay columns, which relate to the window grid. The schemes of ceiling, floor and wall decoration are all defined by this structural and aesthetic discipline. The preparation of coloured images of each bay surface was vital to ensure a line of differentiation between bays. In order to achieve aesthetic control of random damage, each arcade was architecturally reinforced by adding minor details in order to frame the damaged wall surfaces.

At the south end of the building are the rectangular six-and nine-bay galleries, which link those to the east and west. These grouped freestanding columns define a grid of hollow pot domes which rise from arches and pendentives. Each bay was assessed individually to ensure that all fragments of significance were preserved. The form and envelope of the rooms was completed by the south-east risalit and the new bay to the courtyard. A small lapidarium has been formed in the *Bernwardzimmer.*

The courtyards have been changed quite radically since they were originally constructed. Both have been excavated down to the new basement-level promenade and glazed over. The northern courtyard – formerly the Egyptian Courtyard – is filled with a new structural frame supporting a mezzanine gallery and a translucent glazed roof. The southern Greek Courtyard has vast cliff-like rendered walls interrupted by the new semicircular bay on the south side.

The second-floor level of the Greek Courtyard is lined with a magnificent figurative frieze representing the Escape from Pompeii, executed by Hermann Schievelbein. This element of three-dimensional relief is made of gypsum lime stucco and is 65 m long by 1.7 m high, and was originally finished with lead paint to look like marble. At least four different approaches to repair had been experimented with, but each proposal was considered deficient in some way. Again, there was a need to re-ruinate before working up a scheme of conservative and judicious repair, which was able to dispense almost completely with sculptural additions.

The architectural review was greatly assisted by a full-size plaster cast taken of the frieze when wholesale reproduction seemed a possibility. This cast enabled a set of conservation repair proposals that swept away most of the conjectural replacement, focusing and consolidating the picturesque state of the frieze to greatest architectural effect and impact. The severe losses on the eastern range were not replicated to reflect a memory of conflict, while the figurative work was repaired to a level where certainty was provided by the cast.

One quite unique space within the museum is the north-east tower chamber. It is remarkable not only for its height but also for the octagonal plan from which arcaded walls arise to support a faceted, top-lighted dome. Here, two particular difficulties arose. Firstly, the extent of damage, and secondly, the reserve store of figurative panels. The first move was to reinstate the oculus to its original size, which provided the correct lighting level. The second need was to devise a repair strategy for the floor that retained the sense of the marquetry stone carpet but balanced that with a neutral infill where it was totally lost. Next, the lunettes and niches needed bringing into a harmonious relationship with the Brunswick-green arcade. Above that, the main cornice required repair as a damaged but strong element upon which the dome could be borne. The dome itself displayed complete architectural fragments in places, while elsewhere harsh base brickwork substructure was evident. When reviewed at the time of handover to the museum, one can justifiably claim that the whole chamber reads spatially, as well as providing contextual comfort to surviving fragments. The exceptional damage to the fabric by half a century of natural decay has not been expunged.

And so to the uppermost level, where Stüler created the *Sternensaal* in the south-west corner where it enjoys warm Mediterranean light cast on a Berlin afternoon. Few fragments survived – a little decorative plasterwork, some French marquetry flooring, a few walls of old plaster together with sufficient joinery to ensure accurate reconstruction. With great courage it was decided to restore the room, as it demonstrates through architecture the difference between the rational and superstitious mind. The whole architectural programme at the museum is reinforced by this reference to the Gothic.

Above: Pillar placement and ceiling of the Roman Room on the main floor. During restoration the gaps were closed with rendering in various textures, 2008.
Below: View from the Mediæval Room to the Greek Courtyard with plaster frieze by Hermann Schievelbein along three sides, 2008.

Soane left his collections and houses in Lincoln's Inn Fields, London, to the British Nation in 1837, with instructions that it should all remain unchanged from the time of his death. The Neues Museum was not secured by such a legal framework. As a result it has suffered significant alterations to accommodate new custodial programmes in the early 1930s followed by the obscenity of war, neglect and over rigorous stabilisation. And yet it has proved rescuable as a monument to Stüler and Schinkel and all those involved in the restoration, recreation and repair process. The agents of decay have been managed in such a way as to freeze the ruin for future generations to enjoy. It should now be allowed to rest in peace while it regains a patination of age.

XXXI

XXXIII

XXXV

The Treachery of the Fake

Rik Nys

Please assume [...] that there is in our souls a block of wax, in one case larger, in another smaller, in one case the wax is purer, in another more impure and harder, in some cases softer, and in some of proper quality. [...] Let us, then, say that this is the gift of Memory, the mother of the Muses, and that whenever we wish to remember anything we see or hear or think of in our own minds, we hold this wax under the perceptions and thoughts and imprint them upon it, just as we make impressions from seal rings; and whatever is imprinted we remember and know as long as its image lasts, but whatever is rubbed out or cannot be imprinted we forget and do not know.
Socrates to Theaetetus, *The Dialogues of Plato: Theaetetus*, 191d

It is ironic that Mnemosyne, mother of the Muses and the embodiment of memory, who owns all tales and stories, is commemorated by little more than a handful of images from the ancient world, paralleled in modern times with a single painting by Magritte and a butterfly named in her honour. From the abject absent to the surreal and the outright ephemeral, all seem to con-spire to something not worth remembering beyond a mere thought that just slipped by. And yet without her powers, all narration would have vanished, let alone our knowledge of ourselves, our ability to recollect from memory.

In ancient times, poets – having no textbooks to read from – relied on memory, and in an age where records had to be invented, Mnemosyne reigned supreme as the mother of all that could (possibly) be remembered. She stood for divine motivation while aiding her daughters to recollect their routines or particular acts. First there were three and then there were nine,[1] but as the evolution of the Muses in Greek Mythology blossomed, one ele-ment remained constant – as goddesses they were born from the union of Zeus and Mnemosyne.[2] Whatever their number, they presided over the arts and sciences with the intent to inspire those who excelled at these lofty pur-suits. *Aide-mémoire* or spirit of the moment, Mnemosyne herself assured the handing down of a song, a story or a poem, and thus became the patron of all traditions.

While guaranteeing continuity between the generations, she was bound to be forgotten, as eventually recording became a quintessential tool for the

---

1 According to Pausanias there were three original Muses: Aoide – 'song or voice', Melete – 'practice' or 'occasion' and Mneme – 'memory'. They form a picture of the preconditions of poetic art in cult practice. The canonical nine Muses are: Calliope (epic poetry), Euterpe (music/lyric poetry), Clio (history), Erato (lyrics/love poetry), Melpomene (tragedy), Polyhymnia (sacred poetry and geometry), Terpsichore (dancing), Thalia (comedy) and Urania (astronomy and astrology).

2 Before Zeus enthroned Hera, his older sister and Goddess of Childbirth and Marriage, as his official spouse.

progress of humans who, while creating a divide between history and pre-history, invented ever more Gods to rule their lives. The Muses became more independent and self-propelling as the act of recording annihilated the role of memory altogether. Word of mouth was to be taken with a pinch of salt while hard facts – stored in stony tablets – became the reliable source for all that was to be known. It is perhaps for this reason that the marriage between the sciences and the arts was doomed from the start, as the rational became the opponent of the intuitive.

'Arts and crafts' rely on being handed down from generation to genera-tion, and the umbilical cord between time and space provides the oxygen for their propagation. The loss of a tradition, forgotten through the sands of time as the catastrophic result of collective amnesia or total oblivion in a tribal world, is like dry rot, acting from the inside. In mythology, Cronus was portrayed as the God of Time. His personification of time was a force with a ravenous appetite for life, devouring all it created. The cessation of a cre-ative and repetitive process or tradition mirrors Cronus' consumption of his offspring out of fear that they would eventually surpass him. Zeus survived, and established himself as a superpower creating a new pantheon after hav-ing slain his own father. His union with Mnemosyne, prior to his marriage with Hera, is crucial in sowing the seeds for all forms of longevity, offering a lifeline to his extended family.

The Muses, daughters of the patricidal Zeus, King of the Gods, were born at the foot of Mount Olympus and form a complete picture of the sub-jects proper to poetic art in the archaic period.[3] They embodied performed metrical speech: *mousike*, whence 'music', was 'the art of the muses'. In the archaic period, before the widespread availability of books, this included nearly all forms of learning. Some of the first Greek books were set in dactylic hexameter, including many works of pre-Socratic philosophy, and even Plato explicitly included philosophy as a sub-species of *mousike*. Public recitation was a primary mode of delivery and required a live audi-ence. In Plato's Academy, essentially a garden, philosophy was practiced outdoors, as strolling prompted the intellectual juices to flow. The *mousaion* – the shrine to the muses – was found in the centre of his garden, just as the fabled Library of Alexandria, close to the tomb of Alexander the Great, was formed around a *mousaion*. The striking Apollo, god of light, sciences and the arts – party to Zeus' quintessential Pantheon – became known as the *Mousagetes*, or the leader of the muses. As such, he was capable of rolling eternal beauty and the light of knowledge into a single idea while drawing on the muses for divine support.[4]

The arts aside, it remains essential to admit that memory remains the mother of all ideas, capable of creating forms of continuity between the now

3 The muses are typically invoked at, or near, the beginning of an epic poem or classical Greek story. They served as aids to an author, or as the true speaker, for which the author is only a mouthpiece. Originally, the invocation of the Muse was an indication that the speaker was working inside the poetic tradition, according to the established formulae.

4 The age of enlightenment rediscovered (for the umpteenth time) the legacy of the Greek Gods and revisited Apollo and the cult of the muses, eventually coining the universal word 'Museum', allowing the muses to return to their rightful home(s).

Above left: Parnassius mnemosyne, known as clouded Apollo.
Above right: *Parnassus*, Andrea Mantegna, 1497. Nine dancing Muses, accompanied
by Apollo, playing his lyre. Tempera on canvas, 160 × 192 cm. Musée du Louvre, Paris.
Below: *Saturn Devouring His Son*, Francisco Goya, 1819–1823. The Greek myth of Cronus.
Oil mural transferred to canvas, 146 × 83 cm. Museo del Prado, Madrid.

Above: Film still from *Wings of Desire*, Wim Wenders, 1987.
Below: *The Strix (Le Stryge)* grotesque added to the Notre Dame in Paris during
Viollet-le-Duc's restoration.

and then, the here and there. In *Funes the Memorious*,[5] Jorge Luis Borges cleverly allows his central character, who acquires a prodigious memory, to insist that the reference to an object (unambiguously) requires a specific (past) time. In *Great Expectations*, Charles Dickens seems to refer to a future that is bigger and brighter, while Miss Havisham, the linchpin of the story, is stuck at twenty to nine, the exact time when she gave up on life. Dressed for the occasion, poor Miss Havisham receives a letter from her treacherous groom-to-be that she has been defrauded and left at the altar. Humiliated and heartbroken, she has all the clocks stopped at the exact point where she learned of her betrayal and never removes her wedding dress, while keeping a decaying feast on her dining table. Anchored in the past, both Funes and Miss Havisham make us aware of how much we ordain seemingly innocuous chains of events to get a grip on the present and the future.

Come rain or shine, it is not in the 'now and then' or the 'here and there', but in the 'here and now' that we have to act with the heavy burden of decision-making. In the realm of culture, we need to choose between the valuable and the worthless, the meaningful and the drab. Walter Benjamin's Angel of History,[6] inspired by Paul Klee's watercolour *Angelus Novus* (on Benjamin's rather than Klee's terms), has become a suggestive visual allegory or a meditative image – *Andachtsbild* – provoking profound consideration at a moment of standstill. The weight of the present is inescapable, and stasis is celebrated in a halo of cataclysmic powers surrounding the unidentified and the times of yore.

Wim Wenders' angels, Cassiel and Damiel, dwell in Berlin, unseen and unheard, observing and listening to the thoughts of the inhabitants. They 'assemble, testify and preserve',[7] unable to act and eventually growing tired of always observing and never experiencing. Ethereal by nature, they long for physicality, and desire to shed their immortal existence to take part in the present. Cassiel's incapacity to change the past is mirrored by Damiel's promise of a love foretold, and both cherubs combined epitomise our

5 *Funes el memorioso* has occasionally been translated as *Funes, His Memory* as the Spanish *memorioso* means, 'having a vast memory'. Borges explores the need of generalisation and abstraction applied in a philosophical and scientific world.

6 *On the Concept of History (Über den Begriff der Geschichte)*, theses IX, Walter Benjamin, 1940. 'A Klee painting named "Angelus Novus" shows an angel looking as though he is about to move away from something he is fixedly contemplating. His eyes are staring, his mouth is open, his wings are spread. This is how one pictures the angel of history. His face is turned towards the past. Where we perceive a chain of events, he sees one single catastrophe, which keeps piling wreckage and hurls it in front of his feet. The angel would like to stay, awaken the dead, and make whole what has been smashed. But a storm is blowing from paradise; it has got caught in his wings with such violence that the angel can no longer close them. The storm irresistibly propels him into the future to which his back is turned, while the pile of debris before him grows skyward. This storm is what we call progress'.

7 *Der Himmel über Berlin* (1987), freely translated as *Wings of Desire*, is a masterpiece 'in the Age of the Mechanical Reproduction' with a minimal script. It explores people, the city and a longing for love, existence and reality. Damiel falls in love with a circus trapeze artist, while Cassiel, unable to save a suicidal young man, is left tormented by the experience. The monochromatic cinematography by veteran Henri Alekan (who worked with Jean Cocteau on *La Belle et la Bête*) enhances the already mellifluous verbal poetry. When Damiel sheds his wings, he recognises the harsh colours of humanity – this sudden switch however makes him eager to look at the different hues of reality.

humanistic role of caretaking in the built environment. While analysing the baggage of the past we have the responsibility of shaping the physical world to be inhabited by future generations. As custodians, the burden of our responsibilities leads to the realisation that we cannot bury our heads in the sand and wait for 'the storm of paradise' to pass us by. We have to spread our wings and preserve what we have been given by our own ancestors for future generations without tinkering, meddling or tampering too much with the evidence.

This acute awareness – underpinned by shared memory – finds its roots in the last century, although it might be argued that the 19th century paved the way for a deeper interest in our cultural inheritance. As one of its proponents, John Ruskin actively harked back to what proved to be an unattainable (mediaeval) past in ideological and social terms, while his attitude to preservation created an intellectual rift between conservation and restoration for generations to come. His disapproval of restoration was matched by Eugène Viollet-le-Duc's appetite for 'creative' restoration. While Ruskin would exclaim: '[...] Do not let us deceive ourselves in this important matter; it is impossible, as impossible as to raise the dead, to restore anything that has ever been great or beautiful in architecture',[8] Viollet-le-Duc would write that restoration 'means to re-establish a building to a finished state, which may in fact never have actually existed at any given time,'[9] We all know how far the Frenchman – leading many up the garden path – took his own axiom, feeling perfectly comfortable inventing a gargoyle, a tower or a roof whenever he felt the urge to complete his historicist compositions, fulfilling the expectations of many a romanticist.

In awe of the authentic and the original, Ruskin paved the way for an ideological approach that questioned the very idea of restoration, and was strongly opposed to formal interpretations of something that may never have been. In the 19th century, the latter may have suited extremes such as Ludwig II, the fairytale King of Bavaria, who built his ultimate retreat (devised by a theatre set designer), to be paralleled in more recent times by a no less 'mad' mayor of Moscow who rebuilt the Cathedral of Christ the Saviour. The original cathedral (the largest of its kind) was reduced to rubble in 1931 to make way for the Palace of the Soviets that was never realised; Nikita Khrushchev had the foundation pit transformed into the world's largest public swimming pool. The original marble high reliefs were preserved and – though clearly the only surviving historical material – were never reintroduced into the new structure. The current replica now houses modern bronze reliefs that have no precedent in historic Russian church architecture.

It is obvious that the vacant propaganda loved by politicians the world over has little to do with the contemplative image of real progress proposed by Benjamin. Both past and future can be sacrificed on the altar of the present, and neither Mnemosyne nor the Angelus Novus have any value

8 John Ruskin. *The Seven Lamps of Architecture*. New York, Dover, p.186.
9 Eugène-Emmanuel Viollet-le-Duc. *The Foundations of Architecture*. New York, George Braziller, p.195 (Translated by Kenneth D. Whitehead from the original French).

in a world devoid of meaning beyond the headlines of the morning papers. To rekindle a distant memory, like the reconstruction of Berlin's Schloss, will ultimately not mend a brutal rupture in the city – and as in many Latin American countries, it is mind-boggling that modern regimes want to embrace symbols of past oppression (unless you claim there to be no funfair without a house of horrors). Perhaps we underestimate the incredible forces of consumer demand as our environment is eroded to create ever more 'tourist landscapes' offering a franchise of Disneyland in every corner of the world.

Our modern urban landscape is littered with monuments like shells left on the shore after the sea of living memory has receded. We may love it or hate it, but total elimination or reconstruction of our common heritage – Yury Luzhkov style – is somehow easier to deal with, as it remains a black-and-white situation. No evidence is needed at either end, as in one case you eliminate and in the other you have complete artistic license to invent what-ever you designate as factual. But what happens if you have a critical mass left standing that you do not want to dispose of, sensing the burden of its cultural dimensions? Aldo Rossi first described this burden, in 1966, refer-ring to the city as a vast repository of 'Collective Memory',[10] barely two years after the Venice Charter for the Conservation and Restoration of Monuments and Sites was drawn up. The Charter embraced the Ruskinian difference between conservation and restoration, but it was Rossi who made us aware of what it was that we wanted to achieve in the long run with a conscience beyond the self or even the now.

The Venice Charter is phenomenal as it describes preservation while revealing aesthetic and historic values based on the respect for original and authentic material. Its open-endedness, however, is both a strength and a weakness, as it allows room to manœuvre while not being descriptive enough for some. Its most endearing aspect, however, is its ability to evalu-ate an edifice as a document of accumulated time while acknowledging that decision-making cannot rest solely on the shoulders of an individual. Both ideas have been arranged into a single Article[11] in what is already a succinct manifesto, but the gravitas of the argument is more than self-evident. That the individual cannot decide on the future of a historic building is by now unquestionable, but to accept that it can be a document – let alone a docu-ment where all layers of time can achieve equal status – is a different matter. Just imagine that this was written at a time when many a humble 18th-century structure that huddled against the mighty cathedrals of middle Europe was to be torn down to reveal the 'one and only' original edifice at

10 The term 'Collective Memory' was coined by Maurice Halbwachs and later modified by the German Egyptologist Jan Assmann to 'Cultural Memory'.
11 'The valid contributions of all periods to the building of a monument must be respected, since unity of style is not the aim of a restoration. When a building includes the superimposed work of different periods, the revealing of the underlying state can only be justified in exceptional circumstances and when what is removed is of little interest and the material which is of great historical, archaeological or aesthetic value, and its state of preservation good enough to justify the action. Evaluation of the importance of the elements involved and the decision as to what may be destroyed cannot rest solely on the individual in charge of the work'. (Article 11. Excerpt of the original text agreed on by representatives of the participating nations for the Venice Charter, 1964).

the core. The model of Miss Havisham[12] comes to mind, where she celebrates a particular moment of the past – dressed to the nines – while scheming to determine the future of her protégé. She can be seen as a metaphor for this idealised world of a building restored or reconstructed to a particular time, obliterating any otherness or even future development as she celebrates the wedding that never was. Funes the Memorious, her direct opposite, can recall and appreciate everything that ever crossed his path, as to him all memories are equal and can be recalled with the same verve and intensity. In the end, we may feel closer to Funes, but he does not help us to discern where we have to prioritise, as in a building you cannot render every single layer with the same visibility as you can in the world of literature.

The definition of what is valuable has changed from the magnificent monument of a distant past to include the reading of a more recent interpretation of space. On a social level, the moral high ground of the elite was questioned and shifted to include the actions of minorities or those described as subservient to the ruling classes. It is of no surprise that those behind the excavations of Deir el-Medina took a great interest in the community that built the pyramids and less in those who were laid to rest in them.[13]

All in all, it is clear that the times we look 'from' are as essential as those we look 'to' and this gives rise to a completely different awareness of our own position in history. We have to take a position and we have to agree with the enthusiasm of Cassiel and Damiel to interact with what is in front of us. The problem, however, resides in the fact that we cannot come up with a single unifying theoretical approach any longer. We cannot condemn the rebuilding of the Frauenkirche in Dresden as readily as we may like, understanding that it completes the cultural skyline of a city craving to resuscitate a benign and undeserved past. Pastiche or resuscitation, we live in different times and perhaps there is no common idiom that we can all subscribe to.

In 1929 Rene Magritte produced a painting[14] questioning the very materiality of anything we look at. *This is not a pipe* may not respond to any aesthetic frame of reference, but it was asking what the actual painting was made of in material terms. The representation of the pipe was no more than an allusion to the real thing, and we would all agree that it merely represents a pipe as a Platonic idea while in itself it is no more than a stretched piece of fabric covered with rich pigments mixed with oils. But Magritte challenged our preconditioned perceptions of reality; no matter how closely or realistically we come to depicting an object accurately, we never do capture

12 Miss Havisham is a contradictory character in literature and in the context of her time. Her wealth gives her tremendous power, which she uses to coax others to do her bidding and to advance her aims. As she remained in her decaying mansion (Satis House) she moved from protection to revenge as she adopts Estella and claims '[…] I stole her heart away and put ice in its place […]' (*Great Expectations*, 1861, Charles Dickens). Looking like a cross between a waxwork and a skeleton, she does not allow for time to move on and take a different course from the same fate she suffered herself.
13 Jaroslav Cerny studied the village for almost fifty years until his death in 1970 and was able to name and describe the lives of many workmen from the Ramesside period.
14 *La trahison des images* (*The Treachery of Images*) (1928–29) or *Ceci n'est pas une pipe*. Sometimes translated as *The Betrayal of Images*, René Magritte, 1898–1967.

Above: Neuschwanstein Castle, 1869–1886. Hohenschwangau, Bavaria, Germany.
Middle: View of Dresden Altstadt, Postcard 1909.
Below: *The Treachery of Images*, René Magritte 1928–1929. Oil on Canvas, 63.5 × 93.98 cm.
Los Angeles County Museum of Art, Los Angeles, California.

the item itself. Ersatz, counterfeit or replica, we can no longer accept any of them, as the argument strikes at the very heart of the thing itself. What if the reversible 'this is not a pipe' were to stick and what if we can start to appreciate a layer of original monochrome render as much as a bit of plaster imbued with a colourful palette of pigments? What if we can accept a scrap of history for what it really is: physical matter soaked with memory?

To evaluate memory remains a complex issue, as memory talks simultaneously of identification and distance. Just over a hundred years ago, Alois Riegl was keen to establish a memory-value system that should enable us to discern priorities and levels of care for our monuments. Unfortunately, his recognition of historical value in a monument can easily result in the construction of the object as new, and he failed to identify the (aesthetic) category of the fragment. At the dawn of Modernism, his attraction to the new appeared stronger than to the old. He had, however, established that the new had to be distinctly different from the old: 'the truly modern work must, in its concept and detail, recall earlier work as little as possible'.[15] Perhaps radical at the time, he clearly establishes the principle of avoiding the 'treachery of the fake'.

There is a lot to be said about the fragment, though it has not been analysed much beyond the confines of the romantic or the commemorative. Like the limb of a saint, the fragment has been venerated as a relic of the past and was either enshrined or left untouched. The leaving of fragments to the elements would lead to utter decay and annihilation, while enshrinement leads to hysteric idolatry or the entombment of the frozen segment. The nature of the fragment is that it is both incomplete and isolated or decontextualised. As a splinter, chip or scrap it is perhaps more potent, as it is at once distant and stimulates the need for identification. This inherent ambiguity is extremely powerful, as the mind, desperately, seeks to fill in the missing parts. The loss of (its own) context and the will to introduce the new as radically different has evolved from the exposed fragment (Basil Spence's Coventry Cathedral or Egon Eiermann's Kaiser Wilhelm Gedächtniskirche in Berlin) to the entombed fragment (Sverre Fehn's Hedmark Cathedral Museum in Hamar) and the elevated fragment (Carlo Scarpa's Castelvecchio Museum in Verona); all have sought to introduce a second order opposed to and extremely different from the original. From Alois Riegl to the Charter of Venice, opposing geometries seem to fulfil the desire to create an intense contrast, believing that a dialogue with the past can only be achieved with a precise manifestation of the present. The postwar ideology of discontinuity through the accentuated separation of past artefacts and modern technology seems to conspire to trap memory in an oubliette once again.

The 'storm of paradise' cannot be subdued and the march of progress is upon us. The pictorial arts – perhaps less in search of a lost Arcadia – seem to suffer less from the extreme divide between conservation and restora-

15 Alois Riegl. *Der moderne Denkmalkultus. Sein Wesen und seine Entstehung.* Vienna, 1903. (Translated: *The Modern Cult of Monuments; Its Character and Origin*, trans. Forster and Ghirardo, Oppositions 25, Fall 1982).

tion and the will to distinguish between the old and the new. At first, they allowed for mute tones or renders to fill the gaps where bits were missing and gradually allowed for a colour range with lesser tonalities to bridge the gaps. In the restoration of pottery you complete the form, allowing the fragment to sit in a formal (correct) position, while the use of softer tones allows for pictorial continuity in the fine arts. The concept of continuity (using identical geometries) is most inspiring. It may open the doors for endless debates about the acceptability of the 'faux' as it deliberately swings between 'trompe l'œil' and distinctly differently-pixelated parts of a tableaux, but it liberates us from seeking the manifestly different.

To embrace the fragment and weave it unashamedly into a new whole, recognising relatively recent memories, accepting the shrapnel of the past – as another layer among the many – points to a brave new world where it is not Miss Havisham but Mnemosyne who can return and reside in the 'here and now'. The Angelus Novus can spread its wings and the muses can happily return from whence they came while the cherubs can descend on humankind with renewed confidence.

XXXVI

XXXVIII

A Temple of Memory
On David Chipperfield's Neues Museum

Peter-Klaus Schuster

*In memory of Gisela Holan, without whose many years of endeavour at the
Staatliche Museen zu Berlin, the rebuilding of the Museum Island would never
have succeeded.*

Old and new

Nomen est omen – the name says it all! The wisdom of such a maxim
remains true, even when up until recently countless visitors to the Museum
Island, seeing the ruins of the Neues Museum, felt compelled to ask, what
is so new about this museum? This confusion grew further upon hearing
the explanation that Schinkel's seemingly well-preserved museum building
on the other side of the street is actually the Altes Museum, which has gone
by this name since 1855 when Stüler's museum temple opened its doors,
while Stüler's then new building was given the name 'Neues Museum'.
All these confusing entanglements as to the old and new on the Museum
Island now enter into a new phase with David Chipperfield's new Neues
Museum, with his staggeringly brilliant rebuilding and restoration of
Stüler's old Neues Museum.

The rises and falls of history

For over sixty years the Neues Museum was a ruin, preserved initially in a
makeshift way and then with great care. Since its destruction by repeated
bombing in the Second World War it is the only building on the Museum
Island that did not reopen its doors as a museum after 1945. That it
remained preserved at all is due solely to the efforts of museum colleagues
in the former GDR. In 1986 they had a concrete slab inserted under the
ruin to act as a secure platform, without which the building would have
eventually sunk forever into the marshy grounds of the Museum Island.
On 1 September 1989 the completion of this work on the new foundation
and the resolution adopted to rebuild the museum were officially celebrated.
With the first day of September, a date was chosen that was significant for
the ceremony, namely the outbreak of the Second World War fifty years
before. Just a few weeks after this laying of the new foundation stone, the
GDR ceased to exist. Its final deed of importance in cultural policy was to
ensure that the Neues Museum was saved.

Downfalls are, astoundingly enough, inscribed in Stüler's museum temple practically as a leitmotif, lending its name of convenience, the 'Neues
Museum' – *nomen est omen* – a completely new resonance. In a mythical,
aggrandising self-stylisation that was at once typical of the educated
middle class and characterised by ideas of Enlightenment, Idealism and

Above: Neues Museum, ruined state, ca. 1986.
Below: The cornerstone is laid for the reconstruction of the Neues Museum, with the GDR
Minister of Cultural Affairs, Hans-Joachim Hoffmann, presiding, along with the Deputy
General Director of the Staatliche Museen zu Berlin (Ost), Dr. Gisela Holan, 1 September 1989.

Romanticism, Stüler's museum temple was envisioned as the 'Neues Museum' that was to offer the treasures of antiquity, homeless since the downfall of Pompeii in 79 AD, a new aegis on the Museum Island in the very heart of Berlin.

Schievelbein's frieze in the Greek Courtyard illustrates this founding myth, drawing inspiration from Edward Bulwer-Lytton's successful novel *The Last Days of Pompeii*. In an emotive visual fiction on the north wall, Schievelbein shows Pluto, god of the underworld, on the peak of Vesuvius, thus turning the volcano's eruption into an act of divine punishment. Terrified, the citizens of Pompeii flee from impending doom until they and the artworks they have managed to save are joyously received on the west side of the frieze by Ignaz von Olfers, general director of the Berlin museums, and Friedrich August Stüler, the museum's architect. All that the Muses had once inspired in Pompeii and which had escaped the catastrophe has now found a refuge in the Neues Museum. On Schievelbein's frieze not only the salvaged artworks find sanctuary in the Neues Museum, but also the people of the ancient world. If the Museum Island thus appears to be the final rightful destination of Roman art and culture and its learned study, this only mirrors the influence enjoyed in Berlin by Theodor Mommsen, the outstanding scholar of the history of Rome, who constantly compared Roman history to contemporary political developments of the 19th century.

This dialectic between old and new, the downfall of the old as a prerequisite and legitimation of the new, is also the world historical theme of Kaulbach's monumental fresco cycle on the staircase walls of the Neues Museum. Begun in 1843 and first completed long after the opening of Stüler's museum in 1866, Kaulbach's cycle shows the historical development of human civilisation in six pictorial stations as one of continual progress, from the destruction of the Tower of Babel and the blossoming of the Classical age, the destruction of Jerusalem, the suppression of the Huns and finally the victorious crusades in the Holy Land through to the triumph of science and religion in the Renaissance and Reformation, with Luther and an open Bible at the centre. In accordance with Hegel's philosophy of history, this momentous historical panorama assembles those defeats and victories decisive for attaining human civilisation in the present, for the blossoming of the arts and sciences in Protestant Prussia. But that is by no means all – Hegel's three stages of world history, the progression from the symbolic to the idealistic and culminating in the Romantic aeon, was mirrored in the arrangement of the different collections on the three floors of the Neues Museum, from pre- and early history and ethnology, Egyptian and classical archaeology through to the so-called 'art cabinet' (*Kunstkammer*) and prints and drawings section.

Stüler's Neues Museum was a temple of modern historical scholarship. Only those who know history can grasp art and understand themselves. It is in this sense, as a sumptuously decorated, Classical-Romantic shrine to historicism, following the guiding principle and revered vision of the 19th century, namely that different arts and cultures are to be granted the same

Above: Schievelbein frieze in the Greek Courtyard, 1850/51, *The Destruction of Pompeii*, detail of north wall: Pluto sits atop the peak of Vesuvius as symbol of the volcanic eruption. To the left and right the winds lift lava rocks into the air.
Below: Schievelbein frieze, detail of west wall: Ignaz von Olfers, general director of the Berlin museums, and architect Friedrich August Stüler welcome the fleeing Pompeians at the entrance to the Neues Museum.

scholarly and aesthetic appreciation – following historicism's farsighted ideal of tolerance towards the utterly different in history – that the Berlin scholars thus arranged the various settings of the Neues Museum. There was an encyclopaedic display of the material in dignified glass cases as well as the use of the very latest scientific classifying systems. For instance, the recently identified three stages of the Stone Age, Bronze Age and Iron Age in pre- and early history were strikingly visualised for visitors in a series of murals in the museum. Highly momentous for future museum scenography, and not only for the Museum Island but beyond, were the legendary settings providing visitors with a tangible experience of history, illustrated and popularised in lively images. A direct path leads from the theatrical temple architecture in the Egyptian Courtyard to Hollywood, to the opulent scenery and costumes of famous period films from the 20th century. With its suggestive look back at history and, even more accurately, at the various histories of the different cultures, Stüler's Neues Museum was indeed an entirely new kind of museum.

Mnemosyne

This utterly unique museum temple for modern art and history scholarship on a universal scale, where for the first time the programme was realised that was heralded by the inscription on Schinkel's Altes Museum: 'Studio Antiquitatis Omnigenae' (erected to study all antiquities), Stüler's innovative temple of history was not itself spared by history. Quite the opposite: the destructive potential of history unleashed by Nazi Germany ravaged this museum with particular severity. The spectacular staircase including Kaulbach's fresco cycle was completely destroyed by bombs as early as 1943. In the final weeks of the war, in February 1945, Stüler's Neues Museum was finally shelled into a complete ruin.

Downfall as the destructive signature of history admittedly brings to light something inherent in the idea of the museum that is mostly no longer appreciated today in museums, and David Chipperfield, Julian Harrap and their teams have rendered this immediately obvious in the richly faceted, restored structural shell of the Neues Museum. Named after the *museion* as the place dedicated to the Muses, the museum has always also been the place where Mnemosyne, the divine mother of all nine Muses and the goddess of memory, presides. Without Mnemosyne, without the goddess of memory, there would be no Muses and hence no museum.

Due to the 19th-century's belief in progress, the belief in the relentless march of history for the better held by a century so dazzlingly brilliant in the development of museums, this aspect was hardly ever reflected on. No matter how prominently and in how much detail they display the history of humanity, civilisation, art or art history in their visual programmes, astonishingly few museums refer specifically to Mnemosyne. As such, she secures for all the arts as well as for their viewers the remembering look back into the depths of history, to its catastrophes no less than to its volatile periods of bliss. Contrary to history's robust mechanism of progress, here memory is a principle for contemplative pausing.

Above: Staircase Hall of the Neues Museum with view of the fresco cycle by Wilhelm von Kaulbach on the south wall of the stairwell, showing the destruction of the Tower of Babel, the flowering of antiquity, and the destruction of Jerusalem.
Below: View into the Egyptian Courtyard of the Neues Museum.

Above: Main staircase of the Nationalgalerie with plaster tondo of Mnemosyne by Gustav Landgrebe, presumably 1875.
Below: Mnemosyne, plaster tondo by Gustav Landgrebe in the staircase of the Nationalgalerie.

As Pierre Nora has accurately remarked, history is perpetually suspicious of memory, for it continues on relentlessly. In contrast, memory, the act of remembering, lingers, abides, is amazed and stricken; it consoles, alleviates and heals; it stores things in remembrance, keeps them alive. Memory poses the decisive questions, like the fearful question of the humanists, 'Ubi sunt, qui ante nos fuerunt?' (Where are those who were before us?). Or the unanswerable questions Gauguin used for the title of his great symbolist triptych at the end of the 19th century: 'Where do we come from? What are we? Where are we going?' Memory interrogates history and sees ruptures and continuities where history merely marches on, indulging progress.

One of the rare representations of Mnemosyne in the iconographic programme of a museum was to be found in the staircase of Stüler's Nationalgalerie on the Museum Island. On the stairhead, before the visitor entered the *Piano nobile* of the Cornelius Rooms on the middle floor through the dome-covered space, there was a marble tondo with the relief of a seated, pondering Mnemosyne, placed high up on the wall where the stairs come to an end. Each visitor, flanked by Geyer's frieze of Great Germans as they climbed the stairs, thus strode unavoidably toward the portrait of Mnemosyne. Passing her to the left in her viewing direction, in the domed foyer one immediately encountered her daughters, the Muses, which as sculptures on high columns lined the blue dome that evoked the sky. Only then was the museum collection reached, the paintings and sculptures acquired by the Nationalgalerie in the Cornelius Rooms. Here, then, at an eminently prominent place on the Museum Island, Mnemosyne was visible in her double role since 1876, since the opening of Stüler's Nationalgalerie, as mother of the Muses and goddess of memory, complementing the staircase frieze of great men – the great figures are almost exclusively men – who make up the glory of the German cultural nation as politicians, scholars and artists, beginning with Arminius and his victory over the Romans through to the outstanding cultural figures of the time, amongst them naturally the Museum Island builders: Schinkel, Stüler and Kaulbach.

It is an appealing notion to imagine that, during one of his visits to the Nationalgalerie, Aby Warburg noticed this prominent and astonishing positioning of a melancholic Mnemosyne immersed in thought in her double role, and was then moved to follow this example by having the name of Mnemosyne inserted in the lintel above the entrance of his famous 'Kulturwissenschaftliche Bibliothek Warburg' in Hamburg. It was through the ideas of Warburg that Mnemosyne once again became a cult figure of memory worldwide, an appeal that went beyond the confines of art history. For Warburg, the gift of Mnemosyne, to be able to remember, was the foundation for the cultural achievement of art. Warburg observed the recurrence of the same visual formulations in the pictorial works of the most diverse periods and cultures. He discerned in these 'pathos formulae', as Warburg called them and which he collected in a visual atlas entitled *Mnemosyne* that remained uncompleted, the 'engrams of the experience of suffering'. According to Warburg, these are ancient formulae of human body language, gestures and facial expressions, which from time immemorial man has recalled and seized upon to reflect on or master all the emotional states of human existence. For Warburg one of the most precious – because it was one of the earliest – pathos formulae, which he investigated thoroughly, was the gesture of being immersed in thought, conveyed by the head propped up in a hand, as represented on the relief of Mnemosyne in the Nationalgalerie. No less children of Mnemosyne than the Muses, humans, so Warburg's conviction, shape and master their lives through their faculty of memory, their gift of recollection and mimetic imitation of the archetypical pathos formulae of art, which in turn recreate the elementary expressions of the very first humans. Human beings live from memory, which as a repository provides them with patterns of life and expression, also with a view to the future. For Warburg, it is this gift of remembering, Mnemosyne, that first turns man into a liberated species capable of self-empowerment amidst the vicissitudes of history. It is emphatically programmatic therefore that when, following its move from Hamburg to London in the wake of the Nazi rise to power in 1933, the Warburg Institute eventually took up residence in a new building from the 1950s on Woburn Square, just behind the British Museum, there could be found carved into the stone of the lintel above the entrance to the library, as before: 'MNEMOSYNE'. All that has come to pass, including the years from the exodus out of Hamburg to re-establishing the Warburg Library in London, has to be remembered. Nothing should be left to oblivion!

Rooms of memory

As places where the Muses and Mnemosyne congregate, museums are places of memory. Following the enormous war damage on the Museum Island, particularly to the Nationalgalerie, the destroyed tondo of Mnemosyne in the staircase was not replaced as rebuilding began in 1946. But as also set out in the principles formulated for the extensive overall redevelopment of the Museum Island, underway since German reunification, whatever original works were lost in the war are not to be copied – they are to remain lost. This holds for the lost Mnemosyne; nothing in the staircase of the rebuilt Nationalgalerie opened at the end of 2001 recalls her. Stüler's Nationalgalerie gained a deliberately inserted window to history however, a place recalling its chequered history, in the circuit on the first storey. Passing through a picture gallery, the visitor unexpectedly enters a residual room behind the walls, accessible only since the overall redevelopment. Here the surprised visitor becomes aware of Stüler's original and now clad building features. At the same time it becomes clear that the small rooms just passed through are not part of the original layout. Instead, these are fixtures from 1914, modelled on the décor of the Goethe era, which were to turn an originally open pillared hall into an area where paintings could be hung. To transform the solemn temple into a functional museum, the present-day redevelopment has also regulated the height of the once enormous Cornelius Rooms through a newly inserted ceiling, so that Stüler's Nationalgalerie is now usable for the first time as a museum fitted with modern technology on all floors. The curators responsible for historical preservation were willing to compromise here, for the changes are so subtle that they are barely noticeable.

Above: Entrance to the Kulturwissenschaftliche Bibliothek Warburg in Hamburg, ca. 1926.
Below: *Window onto History* on the ground floor of the Alte Nationalgalerie in Berlin.

In the Bode Museum, the second building that has undergone an overall redevelopment, which was reopened in autumn 2006, the loss of the past is even less noticeable. On the contrary, even more so than in Stüler's Nationalgalerie, in the Bode Museum, the restored former Kaiser Friedrich Museum, it seems that we encounter the past as recovered time. Despite all the destruction inflicted in the war's final weeks, and thanks to the unobtrusive restorative work undertaken in the GDR, the original building structure was by and large preserved to such an extent that its surfaces could be meticulously repaired and cleaned. The décor elements, such as the historicising timber ceilings, were restored, while work on completely renewing the stucco ceilings – obviously renewed in the 1920s – was carried out within a strictly set framework. Given the large expanses that remained, completing the marble and terrazzo floors proved unproblematic. Contributing decisively to the impression of a recovered past is however the presentation of the collections, which is oriented on Bode's ideas and embraces all genres. The outcome is not a special museum for sculptures and paintings, but once again an atmospheric museum amidst the architectural spoils acquired by Bode and largely preserved. It is as if history has come to a halt, as if no time has transpired. Today still fully in accord with Bode's artistic museum dramaturgy, a Wilhelminian neo-Baroque architecture exuding power and prestige alternates with a Florentine Renaissance basilica and, following suddenly, a Prussian Rococo staircase. Here the Bode Museum reveals itself unchanged as a child of museum historicism, staged on the Museum Island so suggestively and eruditely for the first time with Stüler's Neues Museum.

But where the war has dug deep scars in the walls, for instance the exterior of the Pergamon Museum or the columns of the colonnade courtyard, we can observe how artists from all over the world have paid attention to the catastrophe of history, as a sign of the irritating fascination and meditative awe felt when faced with the destructive violence of history. Steve Steinman from Los Angeles is one example, who during his years in Berlin discovered the Museum Island as a place of remembrance. With charcoal Steinman rubs the imprint of the shell-pocked walls of the Pergamon Museum onto thin canvas, which enables him to fix the explosions of history inscribed in the stone of the Museum Island as a black-and-white frottage.

But what if – as in Stüler's Neues Museum – not only are the walls destroyed by war, but entire sections obliterated, if there remains only a view of a void? This is precisely the task that David Chipperfield saw himself faced with. It is of course possible to rebuild everything anew, even in the old style. During the years of the GDR, reference pieces were collected of all the destroyed sections which probably could have served as a basis for reconstruction. A brand new old Neues Museum would have been the result, but then the genuinely old preserved in its original state – and despite the ruinous overall state of Stüler's Neues Museum there is astoundingly a great deal – would no longer have been recognisable. The result would have been a new-old pastiche that would have disavowed every vestige of the past. Such an approach, allowing all that is old to look as if it were new, denies the genuinely original its true age, its aura and its dignity. Treated in this way history

Above: 'Justi additions' on the ground floor of the Alte Nationalgalerie in Berlin, ca. 1914.
Below: First Cornelius Room, Alte Nationalgalerie in Berlin, 1903.

Above: View of the former First Cornelius Room on the middle floor of the
Alte Nationalgalerie, condition after general restoration in 2001.
Below: Bode Museum, Berlin. Great Dome Hall, after general restoration in 2006.

Above: Bode Museum, Berlin. Small Dome Hall, after general restoration in 2006.
Below: Bode Museum, Berlin. Basilica, after general restoration in 2006.

becomes nothing, becomes a gaping void. One cannot deal with historical buildings in a more unhistorical way!

David Chipperfield and his Berlin office under Eva Schad, Martin Reichert and Alexander Schwarz, advised by a host of experts from the fields of monument preservation and building construction with practical experience of the situation in Berlin but also in Venice and Britain, at once irritated and inspired by the regulations set out by the building authorities and the never-ending stream of wishes from the museum side – they have all played their part in transforming Stüler's Neues Museum. A temple of memory has emerged out of what was once the temple of a progressive faith in history. On the Museum Island Mnemosyne has once again found a 'home', where history is neither sentimentalised nor corrected but perceivable in all its shadings, graphically venerable and perilous. The resplendently colourful optimistic faith in progress that once shimmered from Kaulbach's fresco cycle, the belief that the world always changes for the better – Hegel's philosophy of history as the best of all possible worlds – turns into sheer mockery in the face of the staircase gutted by bombs in Stüler's Neues Museum. And yet Chipperfield's emotively minimalist staircase, following Stüler's proportions and gradient, is nothing less than a powerful manifestation of the new in the very heart of the ruins of downfall. Once again drawing on the minimalist formal repertoire of Modernism, Chipperfield's transformation of Stüler's open truss into an immense, enigmatically sombre sculpture recalls the irrecoverable richness of Stüler's once so playfully exuberant Rococo antiquity. Downfall – given a positive turn by Stüler, this archaeological leitmotif for the programme of his Neues Museum as a Noah's Ark of preservation at the centre of a unique cluster of culture and education in the heart of Berlin, this risky central motif of downfall in history, in the face of which the museum seemed to be the sole redeemer – had drastically turned against the museum itself in his own Neues Museum. Downfall had hit close to home here and Chipperfield's architecture bears this demise in remembrance.

As Joseph Rykwert remarks in his essay here, we no longer believe in the grand, all-enveloping systems of history, an Archimedean point from where everything can be viewed optimistically. Nothing was more formative for the 20th century than the experience of dismemberment, fragmentation, parataxis. In 1939 Walter Benjamin noted – it seems after perusing a French book of emblems – that, always looking backwards, the angel of history only sees ruins. According to Benjamin though, this angel is driven relentlessly forward into the future – as in the emblematic representations of Chronos/Saturn as the god of time – and so beholds nothing but ruins heaping up behind him. Given his personal experiences and philosophical analysis of the disastrous course of history, it would be frivolous to want to dismiss Benjamin as being an incorrigible Romantic infatuated by ruins. And this holds for David Chipperfield Architects too; involved in building projects across the globe, ruin Romanticism is not a category informing their approach. Instead, their rebuilding of the Neues Museum considers a museum temple that not only exhibits artefacts of history but on and in which history itself has dramatically left its mark. Chipperfield's rebuilding of Stüler's Neues Museum creates a completely new, self-reflective temple to history. Its architectural vocabulary of forms and its design visualise for each and every visitor, forcefully and pointedly, the impact of history no less than the actual museum exhibits, fostering our collective memory and insight into the power and powerlessness of humans in the face of history.

The miracle of Chipperfield's Neues Museum lies however in the paradox of grandeur and an almost Arcadian serenity, through which even the most earnest of thoughts gains a form. Just as the houses in Pompeii bearing all the marks of the catastrophe are still able to enchant us today, in Chipperfield's Neues Museum what once was, is brought out sumptuously, the presence of the saved shimmers through everywhere, the exhilarating spell of amazement at how all this could have possibly survived the inferno. This joy and cheerfulness extends through the whole building, for, after their careful cleaning and feasible restoration, the destroyed surroundings were harmonised empathetically with the surviving original state. Only such a judicious approach could prevent the whole undertaking from slipping into the poles of what had to be absolutely avoided: the crassly arranged patchwork of old and new on the one hand, which renders impossible any calm presentation and viewing of the exhibited works, or the homogenising pastiche on the other, through which everything appears either to be shiningly new or sham old and thus unmemorable. Instead, in Chipperfield's Neues Museum there is a filigree diversity of perspectives, a multiperspectivity that treats what once was and what is now according to the venerable aesthetic principle of *concinnitas*, harmonious arrangement. Although different, old and new are not distinguished starkly, apart from in the spectacular staircase, but are attuned to a single comparable sound. To achieve this consonance between rooms preserved in such different states, the decision to complement the historical floors as a repetitive décor throughout, as had already been realised in refurbishing the Nationalgalerie and Bode Museum, turned out to be astute: as one moves through the museum rooms, a sense of well-being takes hold, coupled with an amazement at how much public luxury the Museum Island held ready for its visitors from the outset.

In interaction with Stüler, Chipperfield's Neues Museum develops a rich diversity of surprisingly elegant perspectives, which are captured and rendered appreciable with crystalline brilliance in the mysterious photographs of Candida Höfer. What also becomes visible in Höfer's transformation of the former temple of historical disciplines into a temple of memory is how a hovering sense of irreality emerges out of the interplay between new and old architecture. Höfer's photographs emphatically convey how the purified frescos in Chipperfield's diaphanous architecture of the new Egyptian Courtyard illuminate and seem to enticingly salute the viewer. Nothing is more conducive to fostering memory than this interlocking of hitherto separated layers of space and representation. In these translucent rooms, which beg to be shown and seen together, the Neues Museum suddenly develops a new narrative richness, one which, in the otherworldly colour photographs of Candida Höfer, makes Stüler's museum temple with its still splendidly opulent and detailed décor and exquisite and precious material surfaces seem

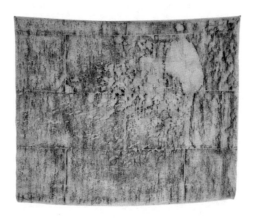

Above: Steven Steinman, *Shroud of Berlin, Pergamon Museum I*, charcoal on canvas, 2007.
Below: War-scarred façade of the Pergamon Museum, 2007.

Above: View of the war-ravaged Staircase Hall of Stüler's Neues Museum, ca. 1990.
Below: *Histoire* – the writing of history, Gravelot, Cochin, *Iconologie* 1781.

Above: The 'Dome Area' in Sir John Soane's Museum, London. Sir John Soane, watercolour on paper, 22.1 × 33.6 cm, 1825.
Below: Room of the Niobids in the Neues Museum, detail of south wall with caryatid porch and tablet inscribed with quote from Sophocles.

like a distant relative of the no less historical fairytale castles of Ludwig II of Bavaria.

Casting a look back into the history of architecture reveals though that Chipperfield's Neues Museum has a close relative in the private museum that Sir John Soane had built in London around 1800 for his archaeological collections and architectural work. This was a Classical-Romantic museum as art and curiosity cabinet, which Soane, through infinitely unfurling visual axes, lent a Piranesi-like shift in perspectives on the relics he had gathered from the arts and cultures of the world. Here world history appears as an elaborate fragment of a totality, ungraspable and yet capable of being sensed, whose universal impact fills the visitor of its exhibited parts with astonishment, admiration and awe. To show Chipperfield's plans and his different concepts of 'restoration, repair and intervention' for Stüler's Neues Museum at Sir John Soane's Museum was therefore more than just a brilliant idea. It was a way of highlighting an elective affinity across centuries. This also holds for Chipperfield's new constructions in the Neues Museum, for both the classical blocks of the west wing, oriented in its proportions as well as its organisational system on the old, as well as for the rigidly geometrical east quadrant. In particular the dome room of this east quadrant recalls the stereometry of the architecture of the French Revolution and the rigid Classicism of John Soane's famous Bank of England. A cosmos of associations, a temple of memory in the new as well!

Asked by the *Frankfurter Allgemeine Zeitung* newspaper which living person or historical figure he reveres the most, Werner Haftmann, the first director of the Neue Nationalgalerie, answered: 'Mnemosyne'. In his *Skizzenbuch. Zur Kultur der Gegenwart*, published in 1960, Haftmann collected addresses and essays dealing with post-war art and culture and, expressly evoking Warburg, described Mnemosyne as the tutelary goddess of cultural memory, who continued to have an effect even in the war and post-war years. The art of Modernism by no means renounces tradition; indeed it arose – as Haftmann emphasised, not without a touch of pathos, at the opening of the first *documenta* exhibition he conceived in 1955 – 'in the shadow of Mnemosyne, who for the Ancients was the mother of the Muses'. And in an essay entitled 'Über das Humanistische bei Paul Klee' from 1948, Haftmann had extolled the virtue and vitality of memory in even more glowing terms, the culturally formative power of which Marcel Proust, Henri Bergson and Aby Warburg had focused on in the 20th century. Once again referring to Warburg, Haftmann claims that the spiritual dimension of contemporary art remains 'in "memory", in the realm of Mnemosyne, who was the mother of the Muses in the theogonies of the ancients. Memory, which can reach back to distant mythical realms, to the 'dead and the unborn' as Klee says. Sometimes we say: things seem more beautiful when we remember them. Memory thus begets beauty. It begets more! It forms something legendary out of elements of facts and fiction! It elevates things and events into the mythical'.

That Mnemosyne, that the art of remembering, is inseparable from the arts of the Muses, that great art always contributes to this art of remembering while also emerging out of it, as Warburg and Haftmann –

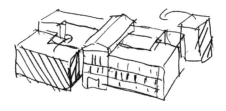

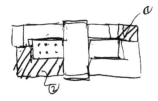

RE-ESTABLISHMENT OF FORM + FIGURE

Above: Concept sketch 'Reestablishment of form and figure' by David Chipperfield, 1999.
Below: Planning model of the new South Dome Room in the Neues Museum, plaster,
David Chipperfield Architects, 2000.

his unorthodox follower – emphasise, is not only evident in the Neues Museum in David Chipperfield's architecture, but also in his dialogical approach to old and new architecture. Contributing no less to the art of memory in Chipperfield's Neues Museum are the works of the collections that have found their place there under the direction of the Berlin museum archaeologists. When Nefertiti is placed in a domed room reminiscent of classical Roman style or the Berlin Gold Hat in a polygonal room with a neo-Gothic ceiling, then these are particularly meaningful examples for an art of memory serving the transmission of cultural tradition which is to become manifest in the Neues Museum. With this new presentation of their collections, the Berlin museum archaeologists are not following the grail-keeper approaches of arcane specialist disciplines; instead, the intercultural relationships between the continents around the Mediterranean, already extensive in antiquity, come to the fore. The synoptic gaze of Mnemosyne, the recollecting sight that brings the different together, is also programmatic for the 'Archaeological Promenade' which traverses the Neues Museum along the elevated ground floor. Here artistic examples of the salient themes concerning humanity, such as – in the Greek Courtyard – order and chaos, are gathered, providing perspectives across cultures and historical periods. With this, Warburg's *Mnemosyne-Atlas* is transformed from a book to a comparative observation of genuine originals from very different cultures. Featuring works not only from the archaeological collections but also those of ethnology and art history, the 'Archaeological Promenade' in the Neues Museum represents a return for the Berlin museums, a return to the museum temple that was the first to match their programmatic claim to be a universal museum.

As a temple of memory, as the house of Mnemosyne, the encyclopaedic gaze on world art in the Neues Museum no longer serves an ideal of progress, but rather the memory of the limitlessly rich potentiality of all humans to survive history, not least its catastrophes. The wonderfully enigmatic inscription in Stüler's *Niobidensaal* – 'Much amazement reigns, but nothing is more astonishing than man' – finds its correlation here. With David Chipperfield's ingenious restoration of Stüler's architecture and the imaginative exhibiting of the collections, the Neues Museum has truly become a new museum, entirely in line with the grand tradition of the Berlin museums. This grand tradition has recovered its inspiring masterwork in David Chipperfield's new version of Stüler's Neues Museum.

I would like to convey my thanks to Doris Berger, Stephan Helms, Andres Kilger, Bernhard Maaz, Martin Reichert, Sabine Dorothea Schnell and George Weinberg for their kind assistance, as well as to Barbara and Thomas Gaehtgens, from whose hospitality in Pacific Palisades my text benefited so greatly.

XLII

XLIII

XLVII

Beyond Representation

Thomas Weski

Captured by Nicéphore Niépce from the window of his country house near
Chalon-sur-Saône in 1826, the buildings reproduced on the first permanent
print in the history of photography can only be made out sketchily. As it was
still so insensitive to light, the film material had to be exposed for over eight
hours. But the image gives us an impression of the ensemble of buildings;
we can make out the yard, a tree and the landscape in which the premises
are embedded. The elevated standpoint provides us with an overview,
revealing the spatial relationships. From 1829 until his death in 1833 Niépce
worked with his fellow inventor Louis Daguerre, who was experimenting
with a different image-producing process. Enabling a focused, detailed
reproduction of the subject, the process was patented by the French
government in 1839, who then declared it to be a gift 'free to the world'
and called it daguerreotype. In the same year Daguerre had photographed
the Boulevard du Temple in Paris from a window. The new photographic
technique now resulted in the street, trees and buildings being clearly
recognisable on the original. Two human figures can even be made out –
a pedestrian and a shoeshine. Because the customer had barely moved
during an exposure lasting several minutes, he is captured in clear con-
tours. Everything else on the move – people, traffic – fails to leave behind
any visible sign on the low-speed film material of the time and dissolves
into nothingness.

   Eugène Atget also accepted this technological shortcoming as he documented old-town Paris between 1897 and 1927. Only what is static is visible
in his shots of apparently deserted streets: the buildings, the advertising
slogans on the walls, the squares and the trees. His subjects were popular
amongst tourists and artists alike because they transformed the soul of old
Paris into images. Later the Surrealists drew inspiration from Atget's shots,
for they saw in them a precursor of their concept of art. Walter Benjamin read
Atget's photographs as deserted crime scenes. And the American photographer Walker Evans, who had become acquainted with Atget's views of Paris
during a stay there at the end of the 1920s, divined in them a capacity to tran-
scend their subjects, one that, as it were, penetrates them and reveals their
true essence, their character, while at the same time manifesting a mystery.

   These interpretations prove that photographs of architecture can show
more than merely buildings. Depending on the respective reading, shots of
this kind enable us to go beyond the representation of architecture and gain
a vision of an age, its social relations and its living conditions. Moreover,
they can lastingly change our understanding of the world. Atget no longer
saw himself purely as a producer of images but as *auteur*. In doing so he was

Above: Nicéphore Niépce, *Point de vue de la fenêtre*, Chalon-sur-Saône, 1826.
Below: Louis Daguerre, *Boulevard du Temple*, Paris, 1839.

claiming authorial status for his photographic activity, drawing on the idea of the author in literature, whose personal style unambiguously identifies the writer as the creator of his texts. At first glance seemingly authorless, Atget's photographs are indeed dominated by an integrated stylistic principle that, coupled with the pictorial vocabulary of a documentary photograph, allows both readings: namely as the photographic representation of what is, and as artistic self-expression in dialogue with the world.

The work of the Cologne artist Candida Höfer, who has explored the importance of public and private spaces for over three decades, moves within this field of tension between an objective gesture and a subjective, atmospheric charging of motifs. Zoological gardens, opera houses, theatres, libraries, museums, private collections – places of research, of social contact, of generating knowledge as well as presentation and representation form the key thematic aspects of her work. Candida Höfer was born in Eberswalde in 1944 and grew up in Cologne, where she completed a traineeship at the photography studio Schmölz-Huth in the mid-1960s. After the war – and contrary to the zeitgeist – Karl-Hugo Schmölz had documented the destruction of Cologne in sober, factual photographs and earned a reputation as a photographer of architecture during the West German economic miracle, working closely with architects such as Gottfried Böhm, Wilhelm Riphahn and Rudolf Schwarz. In his studio, which he ran together with his wife, Walde Huth, Höfer learnt the technical skills necessary for her later artistic work. Following her traineeship she studied at the Cologne School of Arts and Crafts before joining the class of the filmmaker Ole John at the Düsseldorf Art Academy in the mid-1970s. When Bernd Becher took up a teaching post at the Academy in 1976 she switched to his class for photography and, along with Thomas Struth and Axel Hütte, was one of his first students.

Together with his wife Hilla, Bernd Becher had worked since the end of the 1950s on a visual register of timber-framed buildings and anonymous industrial facilities, the photographs arranged in so-called typologies. Shot in black and white, the objects are set in the centre against the backdrop of a grey sky and diffuse light. The standardisation of the pictorial vocabulary and the arrangement of the shots into a tableau, which allows diagonal, horizontal and vertical readings, provide the essential basis for understanding their work of comparative observation, which counteracted the oblivious neglect of a special form of industrial culture and its heyday. Moreover, the typologies, the single shots of which could have been made in different decades, function as a repository of time and a document of industrial development, but also as a schooling of sight. Initially categorised as belonging to monument protection, then viewed as Conceptual Art, the Bechers' lifework is today primarily understood as art in the form of artistic photography grounded in a documentary style.

From Bernd and Hilla Becher, Candida Höfer adopted the approach of intensively exploring her subjects, proceeding comparatively and working into the depths. Her initial artistic undertaking was a sociological investigation using the medium of photography of a socially relevant theme that at the time was a new phenomenon: Turkish guest workers in Germany.

To present her photographs, which still represent human subjects directly, Höfer chose the slide projection, at the time unusual in the visual arts. Later, in exhibitions, she showed her individually conceived photographs of a motif group in sequence. Whereas the formats initially remained within the dimensions of traditional photography, and were thus no larger than standard commercial prints, later she had larger prints produced which, by virtue of their dimensions, allow for a more visceral reception. Early on in her career Höfer employed colour photography before it had gained the acceptance it enjoys today. This was not only because of the poor durability of the colour prints at the time, but also because colour was generally reserved for commercial photography, journalism and advertising. Not until the 1976 solo exhibition at the Museum of Modern Art devoted to the work of the American photographer William Eggleston, curated by John Szarkowski, was colour photography recognised as an artistic means of expression and accorded equal status. Eggleston had deployed colour not so much to give his motifs a precise delineation but rather as a factor evoking specific moods, subtly guiding the perception of the viewer through the elaborately produced prints. In his best works the objects point beyond themselves and show us a cosmos behind the visible world.

Like Eggleston, Höfer exclusively used a 35-mm camera at first, an unusual step for photographing architecture. The enlargements seem some-what sketchy, but this imperfection allows more room for association by the viewer than the results of the large-format cameras usually employed in this field, which in principle are continuations of the types of cameras already used by Daguerre, Atget and Evans. Their range of adjustability enables architecture to be reproduced without distortion and converging lines. The large-format negatives, tray-sized sheet films, deliver prints that repro-duce the motif in rich detail, with nuanced colouration appropriate for the material, and in high resolution. With film formats such as 9×12, 13×18 and 18×24 cm, these cameras can only be operated from a tripod because, despite the progress made in film material facilitating greater speed, long exposure times are still necessary to capture the motif in focus and in its full depth.

Höfer used the 35-mm camera because it allows quick and intuitive work in space. The resulting images seem incidental and spontaneous. Formally, these early works have little in common with traditional architectural pho-tography; Höfer was less interested in a precise representation, striving instead to formulate the essence of a place through artistic means. The atmospheric concentration that is achieved through the existing light and the selection of the standpoint – the position the photographer takes in space – allows us to embark on an associative approach to the respective theme. While black-and-white photographs always refer back to the past, and are thus understood as documents of a completed act, colour photo-graphs convey something that is happening now, that is ongoing. We also see this effect in Höfer's photographs, which, besides the exact observation, provide us with an emotional inlet to the respective subject and anchor it in the here and now.

Above: Eugène Atget, *Angle de la Rue Lhomond et de la Rue Rataud*, 1913.
Below: Exhibition space with typologies of Bernd and Hilla Becher. Venice Biennale 1990.

Above: Ruin of the Neues Museum, south-east façade with connecting bridge to Altes Museum, undated.
Below: Candida Höfer, from: *On Kawara Date Paintings*, Yokohama, Japan, 2 September 2005.

In spring 2009 Candida Höfer visited the Neues Museum in Berlin several times and photographed the results of the restoration work, carried out under the guidance of David Chipperfield, on the building so severely damaged in the war. These photographs in the present publication mainly show the rooms after their completion and before the exhibits of the collections are installed. Captured is a brief moment in the history of this neo-classical building, a moment where it has yet to resume its function of serving the presentation of art; instead, in these pictures we are able to observe it in its pure form. The photographer has supported this direct presence of the architecture by employing solely the daylight available. Any artificial lighting to be used in presenting the artworks was switched off. Dipped in mellow daylight, the results are photographs of interiors as aesthetic objects, which we will never be able to see again in this pure form, liberated momentarily from their purpose, once the museum reopens its doors to the public.

Candida Höfer has selected a large- and a medium-format camera for her shots. We notice the technical possibilities afforded by the large-format camera. Positioned centrally in the respective interior, the lens is shifted parallel to the film plane so that no converging lines are evident. These converging lines were the trademark of the protagonists of the Bauhaus-inspired 'New Vision' photography in the 1920s, artists like László Moholy-Nagy and Alexander Rodchenko, who incorporated daring perspectives in their photographs, seeking to disturb habitual viewing patterns and furnish metaphors of progress. At first glance Höfer takes a different direction, oriented on classical architectural photography, the goal of which is to imitate human perception by photographic means and therefore reproduce the objects with straight lines and without any exaggerated distortion of perspective. By using an extremely wide angle, her photographs of the Neues Museum convey an emphatic sense of space that is not perceived by us in this form in reality. By contrast, the shots Höfer takes using medium-format camera are usually square-shaped and thus appear less static and balanced. As this camera is relatively light, it is a simple enough procedure to move it around while on the tripod. These photographs are the result of moving through space, searching for something; they often show views from a variety of standpoints and thus abandon the pretence of furnishing a single definitive photograph. Unlike the horizontal shots of the plate camera, their square format refuses to yield to a narrative interpretation and, by virtue of its proportions alone, which do not correspond to human perception, refers back to its technical character.

Besides the choice of standpoint and camera type, deploying digital technology represents another possibility to combine the various exposures of a scene in a single shot. The result is a series of photographs with a balanced composition of light – a homogeneity we do not encounter in reality – made possible because the planes of both light and shadow are now traced and presented in minute detail. With analogue technology, contrasts of light like these could only be mastered to some extent through an elaborate and ponderous processing of the prints in the darkroom – in colour photography, possibilities for such finishing are limited. Today, digital technology creates an even presentation of extreme light situations and the attempt to approach them by way of the camera. These possible interpretations of the architecture by the photographer are rooted in the solid basis of her individual artistic style. Particularly in the area of documentary photography, such a recognisable authorial signature is difficult to achieve. But the use of typical stylistic devices, their repetition and variation, coupled with the continuous exploration of themes, lead in their sum to works that bear, in both content and form, the clearly visible stamp of their creator and are thus unequivocally attributable to a certain author.

On the surface these views of the rooms in the Neues Museum shot by Candida Höfer with a medium-format camera recall early groups of works where the artist employed the same format. Only recently, a series of photographs of the *Date Paintings* by the artist On Kawara was published, which Höfer shot in their respective individual settings in national and international private collections. Here our gaze is diverted from the respective *Date Painting* to the surroundings. Upon carefully viewing the sequence of photographs in the book, we begin to see the painting as a black hole. It is the starting point for our concentration on the individual interior, and in its repetition also the prerequisite for a comparison with the preceding page. We notice similarities or differences, and without being really fully aware of it, we are analysing the presentation of art, its use and the effect it exerts in private settings.

For his restoration of the Neues Museum David Chipperfield proceeded from the state of the building as he and his team found it in 2000. The museum was thus not restored to its original state from the mid-19th century – it is not a bland decorative reconstruction – but rather reconstructed in a balanced relationship between conservation and supplementation. Chipperfield has translated restoration methods for historically valuable buildings and their structure to his work on the Neues Museum – he secures, repairs and rounds off. The rooms, the sole purpose of which is to present art treasures and hence the representation of royal and state power, combine the meticulous restoration of the existing building fabric and of decorative elements like frescos or murals with seemingly sober materials like the originally plastered coloured walls or the old bricks collected from barns across rural Brandenburg. Candida Höfer's photographs show that the history of the museum has not been erased, but maintained in the very fabric of its structure. With this attitude towards history Chipperfield reveals a strong affinity to the tradition set by Hans Döllgast, who in his supplementary restoration of the war-scarred Alte Pinakothek in Munich, begun in 1952, purposely left the marks of destruction visible. Chipperfield's restoration of the Neues Museum is fully undogmatic and thus reflects to a large degree the architect's subjectivity. Decisions he made, for instance the sensitively realised exposure of the materials, lend the restoration a sensuous aura while honing an archaeological way of seeing with which the visitor perceives the architecture and the exhibited objects.

Candida Höfer's photographs also entice the viewer to become actively involved. Just as the partly 'unfinished' restorations – an imperfection

Candida Höfer and assistants, vestibule of the Neues Museum, February 2009.

deliberately calculated by Chipperfield – animate visitors to add elements in their minds and share their observations with one another, it is these very same details that form the endpoint in perusing Höfer's photographs. In a visual experience that runs contrary to that emerging out of her shots of On Kawara's *Date Paintings*, the viewer first takes in the overall impression of the striking rooms and then eventually arrives at the architect's interventions, which unfurl their impact all the more emphatically.

The present series of Candida Höfer's photographs of the Neues Museum melds two visual types and, in their relationship to reality, the notions associated with them. On the one hand, the photographer's considerable skill serves to document the quality of David Chipperfield's 'soft restoration' of the Neues Museum. The virtuosity in the employment of photographic technique and the privileged perspectives facilitate our reading of the photographs, enabling us to perceive the minutest of interventions and trace the spatial connections. The uniform treatment of the individual light conditions provides us with a formally balanced visual palette from which we can embark on a voyage of discovery. The photographs are exceptional documents of the restoration's results, and as such convincing representations of concrete architectural settings. On the other hand, the images are constructions of reality founded in an artistic photography that is documentary in style, constructions that convey to us their author's individual vision, which is concerned with ethical values like dignity, respect and a considered approach to history. Höfer not only shows the exterior form of the building, but also transcends the restored museum and reveals its character as a place of presentation and representation. Like the architect in his work, who also thinks in images, on another level she allows discoveries, narratives and history to emerge and unfold, offering her work in a gesture of astounding generosity as a foil for our own interpretations.

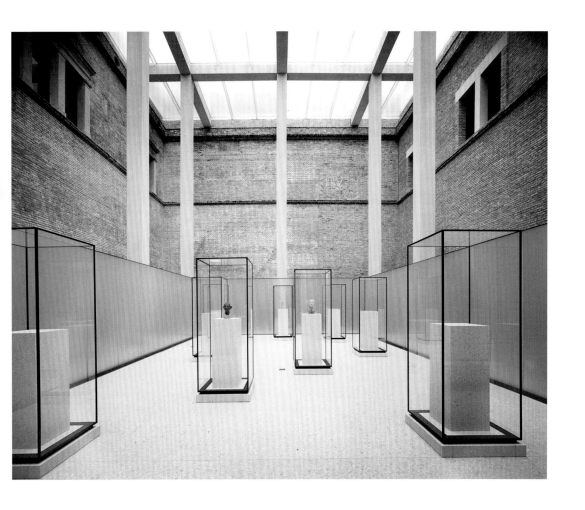

A conversation between Wolfgang Wolters and David Chipperfield

Treppenhalle, The Neues Museum, 17 September 2008

The Neues Museum is part of the Museum Island complex of buildings and collections – a UNESCO World Heritage Site. UNESCO insists on two conditions – authenticity and integrity. Your answer to this specific situation was the reestablishment of form and figure. Where do we find authenticity and integrity?

When we began the project, we were not that well informed about the arguments of repair, restoration or reconstruction, which was not a bad thing. Our first response was an intuitive one. The building had such power, and was so impressive, and we were aware that whatever we did should celebrate this. If you build a house next to the sea you want to enjoy the sea. If you build a house in a big field you want to borrow from your situation. And the context here was not a field or the sea, but a quality of space that was quite Piranesian and almost a geological condition. It seemed to me that the ruin had established its own authenticity. That authenticity was one created by accident and therefore it contained many other stories inside of it – the main story being the intentions of the original architect. So I think that in terms of authenticity and integrity there were two original motivations. The first was that we should try not to lose, through the repair of the building, the 'undressed' condition, which imbued it with a power that a traditional 'restoration' of the building would have lost. Secondly, the remaining fragments were in danger of becoming scenographic and somehow totemic if they were not put back into some meaningful context, because the alternative would be a strange collage of broken and unbroken pieces. Therefore I think that this desire to try and give back a sense of place to the fragment and establish the meaning of the original building was very important in the concept. Those were our intuitive responses, which we started to look at in terms of the traditions of repair, restoration and reconstruction and we found that we were aligned with the theoretical positions.

One could ask about your criteria for the inventions you added to the ruin or to the building. Could you name them?

The dimensions of the damage varied throughout the building, and sometimes that damage was only 10 cm wide, but if you start from the smallest break in the original, you're trying to rebridge. You don't want the gap to be the part that is emphasised.

This is one of the major problems of restoration, not to emphasise the gap.

We realised that when the gap is 10 cm, it's quite easy, when it's 2 m it's a bit more difficult, and when it's 20 m it's something completely different. When it's 10 cm you can borrow from the surroundings but when it's 20 m you cannot borrow any longer.

And the result would be quite different?

Yes, in that it has to have presence. The big gaps are the staircase hall, along with the roof, the Egyptian Hall, the south-east cupola, and the north-west façade. Those are the places where the gaps are too big, and where we felt that we had to contribute. The other aspect is that the entire staircase forced us to ask what the 'gap material' should be when it's more than for example 1 m. We came up with the idea of concrete as a bridge, but a bridge capable of exuding personality in this context.

We discussed whether in the interior the choice of colour would not be over-whelming and whether the old parts would look – as we say nowadays – 'old', and the new parts would look 'new'.

Well I think that was another theme that was important to us from the very beginning. We didn't want to do contrast, we didn't want to say, 'Julian Harrap will do all the old rooms, and we'll try and make really exciting architecture in the newer parts'.

Are there precedents for this procedure?

They do exist – in the Italian post-war tradition, there are some quite nice examples of such a procedure; you freeze history with the ruin and then, like Alberto Molino, Franco Albini or Carlo Scarpa, you add a new element with great care and attention to detail. I think this is an acceptable approach, especially in objects such as mediaeval or Renaissance ruins, which have their own antiquity. However, we were very nervous of thinking that the extent of the damage in the Neues Museum gave us the opportunity to make a radical project inside an old building. I think it's very important for the meaning of the old pieces that the new pieces have continuity; otherwise you have to re-orient yourself in every room. I like the idea that when people walk around this building they come into one room and, although it's a new room, the first thing that hits them is not that it's new or old, but that it's got a different character.

I have another question regarding bridges. In several rooms, new architectural forms touch the 19th-century walls with historical decorations; for example, the niche overlooking the Greek Courtyard. What were your criteria in those cases?

We were fortunate to work with Julian Harrap, because we constantly had a very rich dialogue, and he respected our position. I don't think that Julian would have necessarily done the project the way we did it, and we wouldn't have done everything exactly the way that Julian did. However, there were very good debates among the teams and that set the tone for the project. The debates weren't just between us and Julian, but between us and everybody else – the Stiftung Preußischer Kulturbesitz, the Staatliche Museen zu Berlin and the curators of the various collections. The decision to put back the abside was a problematical one; we found it quite a difficult idea. Julian's enthusiasm really came from the space itself, from these wonderful series of little cupolas and the idea that somehow the space forced itself out and expressed itself into the Greek Courtyard – the desire to recapture that spatial and expressive moment is a very appealing one. As soon as I heard it I thought, 'I don't know how to do it, but he's right'.

It's difficult.

Yes, but everything here is difficult. And what we have done here is set ourselves a continuous series of confrontational issues. It seems to me we've set ourselves up. Setting yourself up means putting yourself in a position where you can fall – you expose yourself.

You invented bridges?

Yes, but I think the richness of the project comes from not avoiding the necessity of bridging gaps and from finding ourselves at junctions and making interpretations. There is not only one story here; you have to continuously refer to different stories and criteria.

It's important that you have different criteria in relation to the place.

To each room, and to each condition; often towards the bigger picture, but sometimes towards the smaller picture.

So you tried to react to the building, and to the rules of the rooms.

I do think that the document we prepared at the beginning of the project, called 'Restoration Strategy', was in some ways vague, but it was philosophical enough to satisfy everybody. It was the right sort of tool for that time, because to have been any stricter at that moment might have been difficult.

Was it written as a political document?

In a sense, yes. But I think it was also a way for us to start to understand the project, because we didn't come with experience of dealing with ruins. We did have to feel our way into the project, but I think one of the continuous experiences on this project is the balance between the intuitive and the intellectual, between the physical and the historical. Sometimes you have to make decisions that are purely aesthetic, and sometimes you're in situations where the aesthetic judgement is suppressed in favour of 'the right thing to do'. I'm not sure I want to say exactly what those situations were, but I feel perhaps on occasion we made an over-aesthetic decision. There were also moments where I think we made an under-aesthetic one, where we could have done something prettier and less 'correct'. It's the nature of this project that these moments exist, but there's no right or wrong in this process. There's intention and realisation, and I think we've been fairly honest to our intentions. I think we've articulated a series of ideas.

One thing I am sure of is that the restoration of the Neues Museum will have, as far as I can see, an enormous impact on what will be done in the future. It shows that it is possible to achieve certain results. Very often we are told that things like this are impossible.

From a technical point of view or a cultural point of view?

From a cultural point of view. But it has been done, and so this project must have – and will have – a great impact, not only on designers, but also on the authorities.

Well one would hope so. I think that, as an office, if we are proud of anything, it is obviously the physical result, but the climate in which the project was completed was fundamental.

This result seems to be particularly important in Berlin.

Yes – without the reigning climate we couldn't have done it. Because we had to have people willing to discuss, willing to have a fight and still talk, willing to support the intellectual idea. I have to say that from that point of view, the process has been nothing but positive and enjoyable. People say to me, 'It must have been a terrible project – you had so many fights', yet I don't imagine I will ever have such an extraordinary experience again.

You touched on the term 'process'. What I experienced during the work was that the process seems to be part of the decision-making.

There was a great respect for our partners. For example, we worked on the staircase for well over a year and proposed a set of alternatives – including a very modern solution that we were encouraged to present. As our partners could see that we were willing to approach all alternatives with equal sincerity, they trusted our openness to enter into a dialogue. Once we had offered everybody the opportunity to examine all the alternatives, we could then build the case for one being preferable over another.

There are probably moments where our hand is stronger, in the staircase hall as we've said, or in the Egyptian Hall, in the cupola, and I think we feel more exposed at those moments – they are the moments where we are risking more.

Maybe the Egyptian Courtyard has been the most difficult issue in the whole project. You had the old photographs, you had the wall paintings.

In a building that has suffered so much loss you can't just repair. You've got to add something through the process of rebuilding. I'm not sure whether in the Egyptian Courtyard or the roof or the cupola room, the additions are more than was necessary. Maybe they are, maybe they could have been more passive, but it's too late – we have done it. My only comfort is that every room has been treated with such a level of invention that there isn't one room that stands out as being 'where the architect really had fun and complete freedom'. I don't think you notice them in that way because every room has a certain degree of intervention. Our responses to some of the historical rooms have been quite radical, while others are intuitive in that they've been pushed and exaggerated in one way or another. I don't know whether the volume of that presence is right or wrong, but I think we can argue our case. The thing that saves these spaces is that the volume of the whole building is already quite present. We often got just as excited, or more excited, over the historical rooms than we did over the new rooms. I can say this honestly, as a modern architect – we never got to the point where we said, 'we like this room because we did it'.

I understand what you mean. What people could ask is about the bridges – or whether they are bridges – between the historical rooms and the new rooms, or the historical elements and the inserted parts. Should there be bridges, are there contrasts between junctions or is it just a dialogue between different characters?

There's a huge amount of manipulation in the stairwell. A lot of people may come in there and say, 'they've just left the old walls, put up some columns and built the staircase'. It is actually a new room and we've just borrowed things and put them back, which is true for the whole building. I would accept that the junction between the door and the concrete is a more difficult moment than the columns and the space for instance, because the proximity, the density, the damage is different. As I was saying, we've set ourselves up for all of these issues, and on a one-to-one basis some are almost irresolvable, so at that point you have to surrender to the idea and accept that some of these moments are really complicated. On the other hand I have to say there are some moments with all of these junctions coming together which are fabulous – you sometimes get a new concrete wall, you get a piece of new brickwork filling in for the old brickwork, and then you get a bit of restored cornice and this creates an unexpected richness. The conditions that put you into that exact place don't normally exist.

And this would be the result of the process again.

233

Yes. It's a story – this building is full of little stories. Going round this building in the process has been rewarding, and everybody who comes here
appreciates being taken through the process. My only concern is whether
you can see the thought that went into everything as you go through a room.
I took someone round the building just before the summer and I realised that
in the finished rooms, or the rooms that are getting very close, there's less
to say and I'm worried that some of the qualities that were there during the
process will get lost. The demonstration of effort is always a futile one, and
a vain process, but I think actually the richness comes through. Some of the
rooms show the process better than others.

*Maybe the major problems in such an experience are the requests of the cura-
tors – what they think they should get and what they feel they have the right to
get. The building functions as a museum, and there are certain standards, for
example for climate, and rules that the architect has to follow – sacrificing
windows, doors and floors, putting holes in the walls, or dismantling floors.
As far as I see, lots of the original windows here were preserved, floors and
doors were preserved, and the ubiquitous fire doors are invisible. What could
you teach architects and curators about how they should react to 'the rules'
and whether they should break them sometimes?*

The amount of work undergone to make the process look easy will never be
understood. Just achieving museum standards in a ruin and not having false
ceilings is quite a feat. We had a rule at the outset of the project – no false
walls, no ducts and no false ceilings. They would have contradicted everything else, but we needed to overcome a few hurdles to get there. First of all,
we needed our client to believe in that concept. We couldn't have said, 'it's
a ruin, a historical building, and therefore the environmental conditions are
not going to be very good'. They would never have agreed to that. So we've
had to achieve museum environmental standards in general terms. The difficult thing was that in order to do that, in terms of lighting and especially in
terms of climate, there wasn't one clear strategy with regards to the building
as a whole, so what might work in one room wouldn't work in another. In one
room you have no roof and no ceiling, so you could bring the services in
through the new ceiling. The next one has a historic ceiling so you can't use
it for the services. That was a huge job for the team – convincing technical
consultants, who normally want a comprehensive strategy, that they would
be continuously changing concepts room by room. That work will never be
seen and will never be discussed – perhaps quite rightly.

*On the other side, one of the results of this process of restoration and your
contribution to the building could be that museum people learn that in certain
situations, standards are standards, but it would sometimes be wise to find a
way – a compromise between what is absolutely necessary and …*

But you know as well as I do that half of the world's great works of art are kept
in unclimatised places. Italy owns a vast amount of the world's cultural

objects, and I suspect that ninety percent of them are kept without any climate control whatsoever. Of course that doesn't justify us not trying to improve conditions, but there are some bureaucratic processes that may be over the top. The important thing is consistency – not great variations in terms of temperature and humidity. We could live with a lower standard, as long as it's consistent. An individual can make that decision, whereas for an organisation it's very difficult. I don't think we've compromised conditions very much – I think we've actually achieved a standard by any means necessary.

It requires the willingness of your partner to discuss things and to accept that something should be done, and has to be done, in order to protect the building.

It's worth doing. You don't necessarily have to change the standards; it just means that to achieve that standard you might have to go off the conventional path. You've got to do a bit more research, and you might have to put that prototype through some testing to prove that it works. We were privileged here, because we had a client that supported that process.

My feeling is that one of the major problems in a building like this, apart from climate, is light. Maybe the changes created by the light of the 19th-century building and of your addition are quite strong. Is there a way to reduce the danger created by light?

The first issue is that daylight is seen as the enemy of the museum, and to be fair to museum directors and curators, they're not completely wrong – daylight is damage, there's no doubt about that. The advantage here is that everyone accepts that this is a house of windows – the rooms look beautiful with daylight coming through the windows.

And the rooms with daylight are the very best for the exhibition of sculptures for instance.

Yes, and I was going to say that the curators of objects, as opposed to paintings, are the least nervous, as paintings have a very different problem. Both for the building physics and for the museum objects we have had to have sun shading devices in all of the windows. There are rooms that are easier and where we can exploit the windows, so in the east rooms on the ground floor we're all very comfortable that we will never put the blinds up because they have the Colonnade. We are lucky to have people like Professor Wildung involved – he's been to every meeting on this project for the last ten years. He's listened to everything we've said; he went into meetings where we put the lights on and then we put the blinds up and he said, 'well, it looks more beautiful without the blinds', and he's really quite courageous. It also means that by using controlled daylight you can get a fantastic spatial connection to the *Kolonnadenhof* and to the Alte Nationalgalerie. There was a discussion at one time that Nefertiti would go in the stairwell as it offers a lot of space. But our argument against that was that we would have had to control the light from the large window to an extreme extent, losing all natural light.

For a moment I will change the subject of our discussion. In the process we quite often discussed or tried to find an answer to whether there is a hierarchy between ornament and figure painting, and there were different reactions to the question whether ornaments should be restored or painted anew or whether ornaments should be treated in the same way as the gaps in the paintings. With the paintings it's a very clear and, let's say, dogmatic decision, and regarding ornaments, borderlines or others, there are different approaches in different rooms. There were lots of discussions about specific decisions, lots of discussions about how the role of ornaments seems to underpin this restoration. For instance, the gaps on the walls in some rooms were painted anew but with a lower level of colour, and in other rooms this has been avoided, though it would have been possible to do following the same rules. And maybe this is one of the questions – whether it's wise to have rules or whether there should be a different approach.

As you know, we had rules that helped to guide us through the project, but also important was a willingness to adapt to the precise circumstance – the overall situation of the room, and the room's relationship to the next room all became part of the discussion. Again I would say that the methodology was totally dependent on discourse – with a group that became experts in dialogue. Its informed and open nature allowed propositions to be discussed that sometimes contradicted our own rules, but ensured another type of consistency of idea. This rigour allowed us to relax the dogmatic authority of the rules, and I think that this was the most important aspect of the process.

Let's talk about the Niobidensaal *– in my opinion it's the most difficult room in the building …*

We've probably made it easier for ourselves by making it a more complete room. Here, there's a sense that in that one place we are giving everybody the room that they can most easily relate to. It's interesting that, during the whole process, this was the room where the competition was judged, where we had meetings, and where we had dinners. It's taken on a special status within the building because it was the most complete of all the decorated rooms. Consciously or unconsciously, it affected our attitude to the room in that we have probably restored it to a more complete level than we have in other places.

This is obviously related to other places, and what I consider very positive is that in some areas you abandoned the first idea to reconstruct huge areas of paint – in the Römischer Saal *for example.*

It is interesting watching a room develop. Something that Julian said at the very beginning, and that we've held onto, is the room-by-room 'idea' – each room must have an 'idea'. It must start to work towards developing its character. It can't just be the consequence of damage and repair; it can't just be what you have left; it can't just be the result of the mechanical processes. Julian said, quite rightly I think, that each one of those mechanical interpretations has interpretations itself. You're tuning every instrument. Every one is a decision. So you have to decide at some point what those instruments are playing, what tune are they trying to achieve?

This would have been a major problem for a less qualified restorer, who would not have been able to retouch or restore the wall to give such an outstanding result. But the top artisan may not offer the cheapest bid …

When we last had a reception here, a member of one of the teams of restorers said to me, 'thank you for allowing us to do what we always want to do and are rarely allowed to'. Until you experience the difference between one thing and another, no one can make that decision because they will always go to the cheapest offer. For example, it's becoming more and more difficult to explain the difference between a good peach and a bad peach. Why would you buy peaches at ten Euros for a kilo if you can buy peaches for four Euros a kilo? You can say, 'but this is a better peach than the other one', but the truth is that it is only when you eat one and then the other that you can say, 'now I understand' – it's only through physical comparison that you can actually compare two things. Our world is taking us away from that. Our world is telling us that a peach is a peach, that a glass façade is a glass façade, that a concrete floor is a concrete floor. And yet, when faced with clear physical comparisons, we can tell the difference.

We have to find the means to realise such a process, and very often, in such a public building, you are obliged to concentrate on people less qualified – you have certainly had this experience before.

Always, that's a difficult thing to explain – you can do a brick wall and it can be absolutely awful and you can do a brick wall and it can be absolutely beautiful, but they're both brick walls, and on the drawing it just says 'brick'.

Could this not be part of the teaching of such a restoration process – that you have to find ways to give the job to the very best people? The way it was done here, as far as I can see, was to describe and to detail what had to be done, and these documents could only be understood by experienced people so it was in a certain sense impossible for inexperienced people to enter into the game.

For me the important thing in life is the difference between things that are not so different. I'm not convinced that we need to invest in enormously complicated things. I think it's more to do with maintaining the quality of what we have instead of fantasising about things. Our world is moving more and more towards fantasy and complexity and away from discrimination and reality, and therefore people can't judge things anymore. I think we have to keep judgement as one of our measures of civilisation and of culture. The ability to judge and discuss literature, the ability to judge and discuss films and the ability to judge, for example, bread or fish. I think the problem is that the world is moving further and further away from quality, and bureaucratically, this is what we experience every day in architecture. How can you argue with a client who doesn't necessarily understand what a good floor is? It's so pleasant to work with clients who are willing to follow you in that way. I have to say, our client for the Am Kupfergraben 10 gallery is someone who has high standards regarding quality, maybe more than most of us really want! But he is so discriminating, that although we found ourselves nearly on the opposite foot, it was a delight. I think we're often not demanding enough and what we end up spending most of our lives arguing for is the subtle difference. The problem – and it affects modern architecture constantly – is that if you design a building and the shape is really exciting and the photomontage shows an incredible fantasy, everyone says, 'wow, this is going to be fantastic'. But if you try and design something quieter and say, 'when you touch this it will feel beautiful', how do they know? It's much easier to sell impact than reality, and it's much more difficult to explain reality before it exists.

It is absolutely necessary to be on the scene the whole day long and to control and to rethink certain situations. So there's the need for something like a professional figure – the role Martin Reichert took here – who brings the discussion forward, and takes decisions about what seem to be minor details. This professional figure, the architect on the building site, seems to be of utmost importance. But should this person be what Renaissance architects called the 'Uomo Universale'? Should this architect know everything, be also a restorer, a specialist for windows, and know lots about technique? Is that what you feel?

This is part of the conversation we had just now. You have to make everything important and you have to convince everybody that everything is important. I think it's true on every project – you have to somehow get the team, the consultants and the client believing that this is a really important project, which is actually something I learned when I worked for Norman Foster. Especially in the early days, Foster was fantastic at making everybody believe that this was the most important project in the world and they were never going to work on anything else of this importance. On this project it wasn't difficult to persuade everybody – we could say, 'look, this is the most exciting thing you are ever going to work on' and it would be true!

But there were big difficulties in convincing people involved in decision-making. And so the whole restoration became something like a seminar – a seminar about values, techniques, concepts and solutions.

I think that there were two advantages for us – the first advantage was that I was an outsider.

Yes, that's true – the outsiders, the people coming from another country, have an incredible freedom, not only to say what they want to say, but to invent ways to realise what they hope to realise.

Our other advantage was that we were a relatively young office – the project was the most important we could ever do and we were bound to take it really seriously. I think our commitment as an office, in the end, inspired everyone else, and I think that comes through on the project. People involved in polemics against the project tended to come round and say, 'I can understand why people are against the project, but in terms of quality I can't criticise it whatsoever'. So in the end we protected ourselves a little bit with the thoroughness and the quality of the process. I think one of the other things that was important in building the relationships that we did was that we gave the people confidence that we were listening.

That's obvious. Listening and having an opinion, knowing what to say about your ideas.

My theory is that if you can't explain an idea, it's not an idea, it's just an opinion. Sometimes you can't have more than an opinion and you just have to say, 'I don't know, I can't answer it. That's what I would do, that's my opinion'. But I think sometimes we disguise our opinions as something bigger.

Opinions and not always arguments.

Thinking back all these years, the number of times we have had to explain the project was a good test of our ideas. We were able to explain, to verbalise in quite simple ways that it's a ruin, it's full of fragments, the fragments are wonderful, they have life in them. We want to put those fragments back in to an order again. We don't want to devalue those fragments by copying them and we don't want to confuse their meaning. On the other hand it's important that we put them back within a context and clarify their position. It's a very short explanation, clear enough to explain the general reason why we were taking this approach, and I think that was key to the realisation of the project.

LVII

LVIII

Appendix

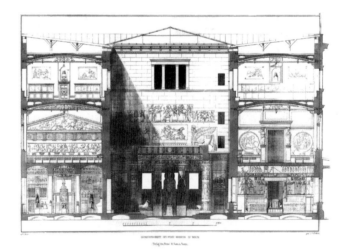

Above: Friedrich August Stüler's ideal scheme for Museum Island. View from the south. To the left is the Neues Museum and in the centre is the Nationalgalerie. Lithograph from: F.A. Stüler, *Das Neue Museum in Berlin*, Ernst & Korn, Berlin 1862, detail of plate 1.
Below: Cross-section of the north wing of the Neues Museum showing the Egyptian Courtyard. Lithograph from: F.A. Stüler, *Das Neue Museum in Berlin*, Ernst & Korn, Berlin 1862, plate 6.

Chronology

1841   *January* – Ignaz Maria von Olfers, General Director of the Königliche Museen since 1839, submits a report to Frederick William IV that proposes turning the whole Spree Island behind the Schinkel Museum 'into a tranquil, richly-endowed sanctuary for the arts and sciences', upon which museums and the university are to be located.
March – Cabinet Order issued by Frederick William IV approving the recommendations set out in Olfer's report.
June – Building work commences: existing buildings are demolished, the building pit is dug and the ground surveyed by sinking wells, albeit only at the four corners of the site; therefore, the precise configuration of the ground was not properly detected.
September – The first foundation pile is driven into the ground; a total of 2,344 piles, the longest measuring 58 feet (ca. 18.20 m), are sunk using a steam-powered pile driver.

1843   *April* – The foundation stone is laid; by the end of the year the exterior walls are erected and the main building roofed. The steam engine used to drive the piles and drain the building site now propels a hoist and a mortar mixing machine, while materials are transported on elaborate scaffolding with tracks for light rail wagons. The technologically revolutionary building site facilities are based on plans drafted by construction supervisor Hoffmann.

1844   Work on the natural stone façade begins. The ceilings are vaulted with hollow clay pots, which are manufactured by the Berlin terracotta firm of Ernst March.

1845   Exterior plastering is completed; window frames and ledges are inserted. Marble columns are added to the interior and the sandstone figures to the exterior of the domes.

1846   Preparatory work for the decorative painting of the interior begins. First officially recorded mention of subsidence cracks, caused by the inadequate setting of the piles, which fail to reach stable subsoil beneath the north-west part of the building. The cracks are cramped with iron braces.

1847   Painting of the rooms begins: the walls of the main staircase by Wilhelm von Kaulbach, commissioned personally by Frederick William IV, otherwise by artists from the Berlin school of Neoclassicism.

1848   Progress is hampered by political events: wages increase, while financing is subject to the approval of the Prussian Diet and, although granted, is not on the scale required.

1850   The rooms for the Egyptian and the Prints and Drawings departments are completed and the exhibits installed. Up until 1860, access to the rooms is via the south vestibule.

1859   The Ethnography Collection is the final department to open its doors. The eastern portico is completed.

1865   *March* – Friedrich August Stüler dies.

Above: The Flat Dome Room following its conversion to the 'Sarcophagus Hall' in 1919–1923 by architect Wilhelm Wille, looking south-east, photograph, 1923/24.
Below: The main Staircase Hall of the Neues Museum decades after its destruction, photograph (before 1986).

1866	Kaulbach finishes his epic cycle on the history of mankind in the main staircase area.
1875	The Prussian-Brandenburg Kunstkammer leaves the museum and moves into the Kunstgewerbemuseum and Schloss Monbijou.
1886	The Pre- and Early History and the Ethnography collections move to the Völkerkundemuseum. The sequence of rooms now available are occupied by the growing collections of the Prints and Drawings Department as well as the Egyptian Museum, both of which have remained in the building, and the Antiquities Collection (Antiquarium), relocated from the Altes Museum.
1885– 1889	The roofs are reconstructed to facilitate the integration of usable rooms, and a windowed attic is added atop the courtyard walls, while the drainage system for the roof is refitted to the exterior walls.
1906– 1916	Gradual handing over of the Plaster Cast Collection to the Kaiser Friedrich Museum (renamed the Bode Museum in 1956) and the Institute of Classical Archaeology at Berlin University (renamed Humboldt University in 1949).
1919– 1923	In a move of historical importance for the museum, the Greek Courtyard is converted into the Amarna room of the Egyptian Collection, entailing extensive changes to the structure. The apse is dismantled, the floor elevated to the level of the ground floor and the inner courtyard covered with a glass roof for the first time (architect: Wilhelm Wille). Access is via the Flatdome Room to the south, which is also rebuilt as part of this overhaul into the sarcophagus room (encircling wall around the columns and pilasters, insertion of a flat suspended ceiling, slit-like windows in the south wall).
1933	The mythological and national antiquities rooms are remodelled in the style of the Neue Sachlichkeit. The original decorations are in part removed, in part painted over.
1939	*September* – The Neues Museum is closed to the public immediately upon the out-break of the Second World War on 1 September 1939. Beginning in 1940 the exhibits are gradually evacuated. Some of the large exhibits have to remain in the building.

Destruction

1943	On the night of 23–24 November the main staircase area is completely gutted after being hit by firebombs. Kaulbach's frescos are totally destroyed by the heat generated from the burning wooden trusses supporting the roof and the water used to fight the fire.
1945	On 3 February 1945 several high-explosive bombs strike the Neues Museum, partly destroying or inflicting severe damage on the north-west wing, the south-west wing, the south dome and the passageway to the Altes Museum. Further destruction occurs as the Museum Island, turned into a fortress, is subjected to a barrage of artillery shelling and direct grenade hits in April 1945.

Temporary uses of the ruin

from 1946	After being fitted with emergency roofing in 1946, the intact rooms of the east wing are used in the post-war years as restoration workshops and depots of the Staatliche Museen; without any temporary roofing, the severely damaged sections of the building (main stairway, south-west wing) remain exposed to the direct impact of the weather until 1989.

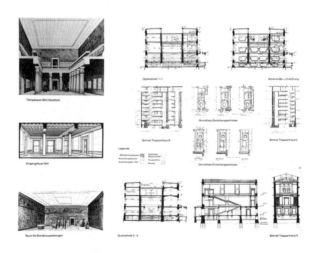

Above: In preparation for reconstructing the foundations, the brick shell of the Egyptian courtyard and other parts of the north-west wing were torn down in 1986–1989. Photograph, undated.
Below: Reconstruction planning for the Neues Museum by the GDR. The perspective views show the Egyptian Courtyard (above left) and Greek Courtyard (below left), undated.

Fundamental reconstruction and structural support

1980   Rebuilding plans are launched by the construction management of the Staatliche
        Museen.

1985   The politburo of the *Sozialistische Einheitspartei Deutschland* (Socialist Unity
        Party of Germany – SED) and – shortly thereafter – the Council of Ministers of the
        German Democratic Republic (GDR) adopt a resolution on the 'general reconstruc-
        tion of the Berlin Museum Island', which includes reconstructing the Neues Museum.

1986   Work commences on developing a technological procedure for establishing
        substitute foundations.

1986–   Extensive demolition – both avoidable and unavoidable – takes place over the course
1989   of the preparatory securing work on the partial ruin, including the still preserved
        sections of the west and north façades, the south-east risalit and the Egyptian
        Courtyard. The south-west wing and the main staircase area are spanned with a
        provisional protective roof for the first time.

1989   *1 September* – At a ceremony marking the 50th anniversary of the outbreak of the
        Second World War, the first of 2,500 micro-bore piles – with a total length of 50,000 m
        – are driven into the ground. Work on the substitute foundations is continued after
        reunification by the Federal Construction Authority and completed in October 1994.

1992   *June* – Commissioned by the Berlin Senate Department for Urban Development,
        an expert commission comprised of prominent figures in monument protection from
        West and East Germany (Ernst Badstübner, Hartmut Dorgerloh, August Gebeßler,
        Thomas Mader, Helmut F. Reichwald, Manfred Schuller, Wolfgang Wolters) formu-
        lates an appeal 'for a complementary restoration' (published as: *Beiträge zur
        Denkmalpflege in Berlin*, issue 1, Berlin 1994).

Competition

1992   *June* – Following a resolution passed on 15 June 1992, the board of trustees of the
        Stiftung Preußischer Kulturbesitz commissions the Federal Construction Authority
        to prepare a restricted competition for 18 national and international architecture firms.

1993   *August* – In terms of the surface areas, the space allocation programme is divided into:
        1. the Egyptian Museum with the papyrus collection (5,300 m^2), 2. the Museum for
        Pre- and Early History (3,600 m^2), the Museum of Near Eastern Antiquities (3,600 m^2),
        an area for special exhibitions (670 m^2) as well as educational facilities (300 m^2).
        The following tasks were formulated as the competition remit:
        Complementing the partially destroyed Neues Museum, including the necessary
        extensions in the area of the Kupfergraben.
        Construction, or reconstruction, of connecting passageways to the Pergamon Museum.
        Construction, or reconstruction, of a connection between the Neues and Altes Museum.

1994   *March* – The international jury chaired by Max Bächer convenes from 14 to 16 March.
        Giorgio Grassi from Milan wins first prize, followed in ranking order by David
        Chipperfield Architects/London, Francesco Venezia/Naples, Frank O. Gehry/Santa
        Monica and Axel Schultes/Berlin.

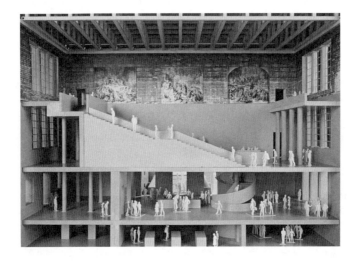

Above: Competition for the Neues Museum with supplementary and connecting buildings on Kupfergraben, massing models by David Chipperfield Architects, 1993–94.
Below: Review and advisory procedure, phase 2, competition entry by David Chipperfield Architects, model of central risalit with Staircase Hall, 1997.

Review and advisory procedure

1994– The building's future occupants are not entirely convinced by the design submitted
1997   by the winner. Even after reworking the original plans, concerns remain as to the
       feasibility of Giorgio Grassi's design for a functioning museum. The board of trustees
       therefore authorises the president of the Stiftung Preußischer Kulturbesitz to initiate a
       review and advisory procedure whereby the five architects awarded prizes are to submit
       new proposals. The remit is now limited to the rebuilding and restoration of the Neues
       Museum in its old volume but now with the additional function of being a main entry to
       the Museum Island with connections to the Altes Museum and the Pergamon Museum.
       The additions on the Kupfergraben side are abandoned for the time being. The scope of
       the space allocation programme is considerably reduced. The spaces originally desig-
       nated for the Museum of Near Eastern Antiquities, special exhibitions and the educa-
       tional facilities as well as parts of the service and depot areas are omitted.

1997   *May* – The advisory body unanimously decides to exclude three architects from further
       consideration and asks Frank O. Gehry/Santa Monica and David Chipperfield/London
       to further modify their plans. Considerable doubts still remain on issues of historic
       preservation and the feasibility for a functioning museum. Both offices are therefore
       invited to submit revised proposals by 27 October 1997.

Commissioning of David Chipperfield Architects

1997   *December* – Following the recommendation of the advisory body, the board of trustees
       of the Stiftung Preußischer Kulturbesitz decides to commission the London architect
       David Chipperfield with the plans to rebuild the Neues Museum.

1998   *January* – Basic evaluation commences (user requirements, allocation planning,
       historic preservation guidelines). Planning studies are undertaken.
       A 'Planungsgruppe Museumsinsel Berlin' (Hilmer & Sattler, Heinz Tesar, David
       Chipperfield Architects) under the direction of David Chipperfield Architects is
       commissioned with elaborating a master plan for the coordinated restoration and
       further development of the Museum Island. The key components are to provide a
       main circuit in the Pergamon Museum, to link the historic buildings with the
       'Archaeological Promenade' and to offer an additional visitor and infrastructure
       building (New Entrance Building) on the vacant plot between the Neues Museum
       and the Kupfergraben canal.

1999   *January* – Work commences on the preliminary planning.
       September – Work commences on the final design planning.
       December – As part of the Museum Island complex the Neues Museum is declared
       a UNESCO World Heritage Site.

2000   *12 February* – The current state of planning is presented and discussed at a public
       symposium held by the TU Berlin under the auspices of Prof. Dr. Wolfgang Wolters.
       autumn – The exhibition *Masterplan Museumsinsel – Ein europäisches Projekt*
       presents the state of planning to the public for the first time (Neues Museum,
       23 Sept. to 5 Nov. 2000).

2001   *February* – The budget proposal 'Wiederaufbau Neues Museum' of 230 million euros
       is officially approved.
       November – Work commences on the construction documentation.

2002   Restorative securing prepares the ruin for future building work.

Above: Queen Elizabeth II visits the building site of the Neues Museum on 3 November 2004. David Chipperfield explains the reconstruction plans using a concept model. To the left is the Lord Mayor of Berlin, Klaus Wowereit.
Below: James Simon Gallery according to the plan by David Chipperfield Architects, view from the Schlossbrücke, 2007.

2003   *24 June* – The commencement of building work is marked by an official ceremony.
        25 June – An 'Open Day' (*Ein letzter Blick*) with an accompanying exhibition showing
        the plans for the reconstruction is held.

2004   *12 September* – David Chipperfield gives a lecture explaining the concept behind the
        designs on the occasion of the '5. Denkmalsalon' in the Rotes Rathaus (European
        Heritage Day).
        3 November – Her Majesty Queen Elizabeth II of the United Kingdom of Great Britain
        and Northern Ireland and His Highness Prince Philip Duke of Edinburgh visit the
        construction site of the Neues Museum during their fourth state visit to the Federal
        Republic of Germany.

2005   *December* – Construction work begins.

2007   *21 September* – Topping out ceremony held, followed by three 'Open Days' attracting
        25,000 visitors.

2008   *June* – The exhibition *Neues Museum – Restoration, Repair and Intervention* is held
        at Sir John Soane's Museum in London.

2009   *5 March* – An official ceremony with a symbolic handing over of the keys marks
        the completion of the building. Three Open Days (*Ein erster Blick*) and *Dialoge 09*,
        a dance project by Sascha Waltz & Guests, attract almost 50,000 visitors.
        30 April – His Royal Highness the Prince of Wales and the Duchess of Cornwall
        visit the Neues Museum as part of a state visit to the Federal Republic of Germany.
        16 October – Opening of the Neues Museum.
        November – Work commences on the new entrance building, the James Simon Gallery.

Site plan

100m

Floor plan level 0

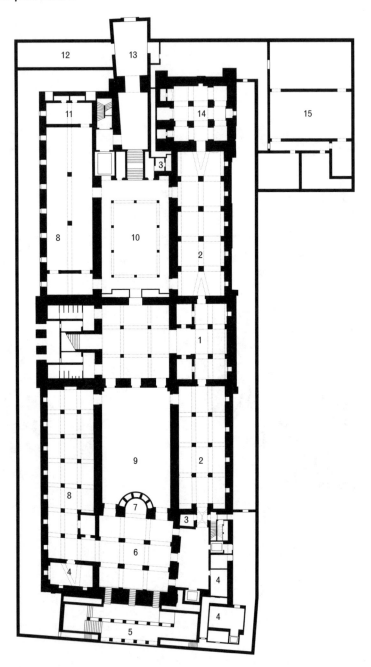

1 Room underneath the Vestibule
2 East Wing
3 Technical area
4 Storage
5 Connection to the Altes Museum
6 South Wing
7 Apse
8 West Wing
9 Greek Courtyard
10 Egyptian Courtyard
11 Education
12 Connection to the New Entrance Building
13 Connection to the Pergamon Museum
14 Treasure Chamber
15 Mechanical Equipment

Floor plan level 1

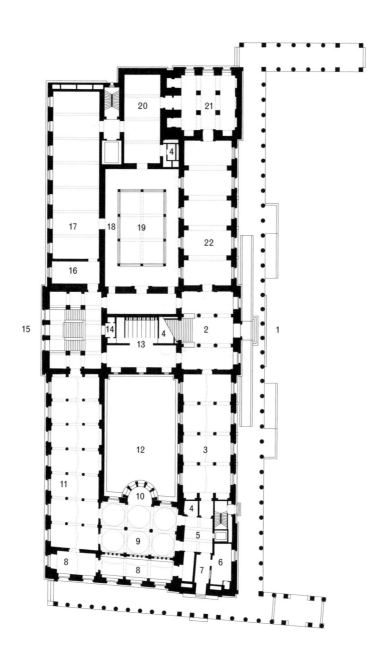

1 Main Entrance	9 Flat Dome Room	17 Historical Room
2 Vestibule	10 Apse	18 Gallery Egyptian Courtyard
3 Fatherland Room	11 Ethnographical Room	19 Egyptian Courtyard (void)
4 Technical Area	12 Greek Courtyard (void)	20 Hypostyle
5 South Vestibule	13 Cloakroom	21 Tomb Room
6 Security	14 Information	22 Mythological Room
7 Employees' Entrance	15 West Entrance	
8 Café	16 Museum Shop	

Floor plan level 2

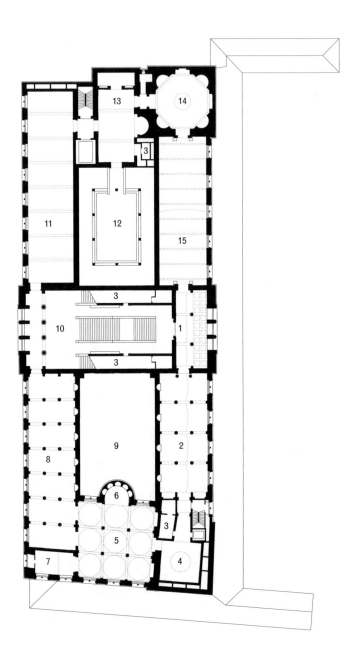

1 Bacchus Room
2 Roman Room
3 Technical Area
4 South Dome Room
5 Mediæval Room
6 Apse
7 Bernward Room
8 Renaissance Room

9 Greek Courtyard (void)
10 Staircase Hall
11 Greek Room
12 Platform Egyptian Courtyard
13 Apollo Room
14 North Dome Room
15 Room of the Niobids

Floor plan level 3

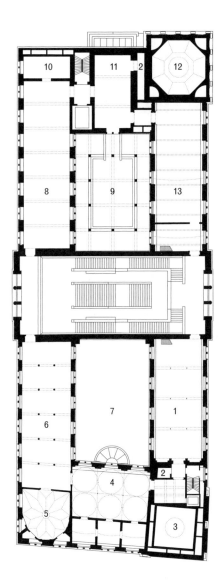

1 Eastern Art Chamber
2 Technical Area
3 South Dome Room (void)
4 Majolika Room
5 Star Room
6 Western Art Chamber
7 Greek Courtyard (void)
8 Blue Room

9 Egyptian Courtyard (void)
10 Education
11 Green Room
12 North Dome Room (void)
13 Red Room

Floor plan level 4

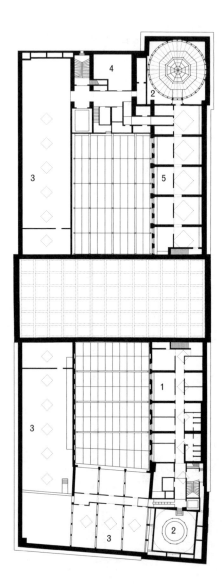

1 Personnel
2 Maintenance Room
3 Technical Area
4 Storage
5 Administration

10m

Floor plan with section lines

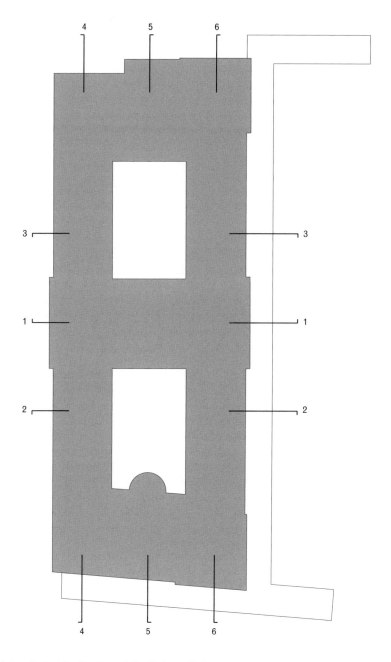

1 Longitudinal Section through the Staircase Hall
2 Cross Section through the Greek Courtyard
3 Cross Section through the Egyptian Courtyard
4 Longitudinal Section through the West Wing
5 Longitudinal Section through the Courtyards and the Staircase Hall
6 Longitudinal Section through the East Wing

Longitudinal Section through the Staircase Hall

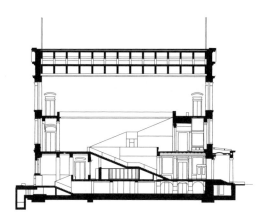

Cross Section through the Greek Courtyard

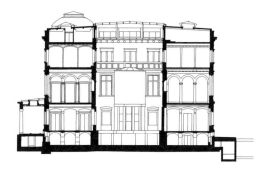

Cross Section through the Egyptian Courtyard

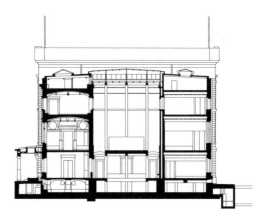

Longitudinal Section through the West Wing

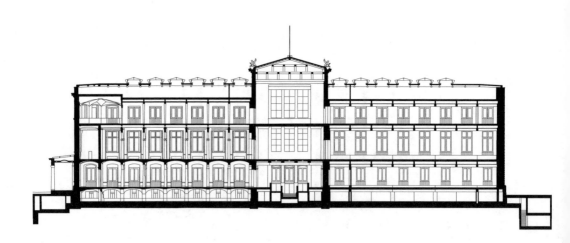

Longitudinal Section through the Courtyards and the Staircase Hall

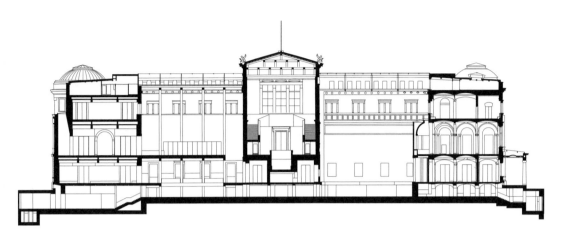

Longitudinal Section through the East Wing

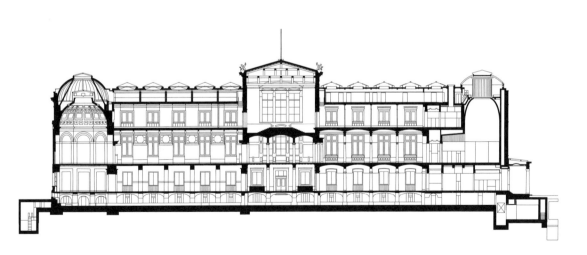

East Elevation

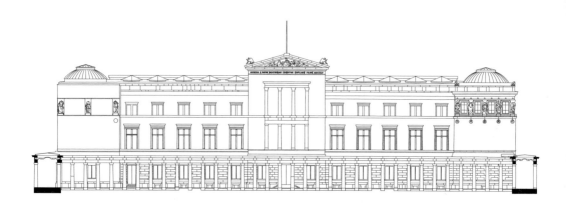

West Elevation

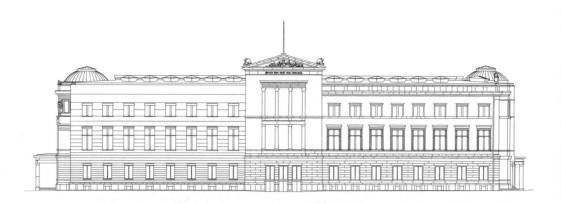

South Elevation

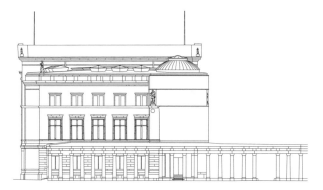

North Elevation

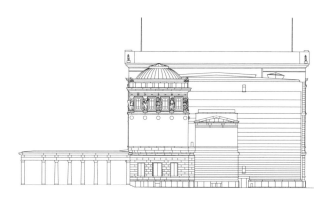

10m

Project credits

Client
Stiftung Preußischer Kulturbesitz represented by
Bundesamt für Bauwesen und Raumordnung (BBR)
Projektreferat Museumsinsel.
Lothar Fehn-Krestas (project management until 2002)
Eva Maria Niemann (project management since 2002)

Occupant
Staatliche Museen zu Berlin
represented by Gisela Holan

Architect
David Chipperfield Architects

Principal
David Chipperfield

Competition, Phase 1

Team
Renato Benedetti, Jan Coghlan, Eamon Cushanan,
Jamie Fobert, Madeleine Lambert, Genevieve Lilley,
Jonathan Sergison, Steven Shorter, Zoka Skorup,
Simon Timms

Competition, Phases 2+3

Project Architect
Mark Randel

Team
Philipp Auer, Franz Borho, Nathalie Bredalla,
An Fonteyne, Robin Foster, Mario Hohmann,
Martin Kley, Harvey Langston-Jones, Patrick
McInerney, Ian McKnight, Claudia Marx,
Guy Morgan-Harris, Rik Nys, Eva Schad,
Alexander Schwarz, Haewon Shin, Graham Smith,
Henning Stummel, Giuseppe Zampieri,
Mark Zogrotzski

Outline Proposals

Directors
Harald Müller, Eva Schad

Project Architect
Eva Schad

Team
Isabel Karig, David Saik, Alexander Schwarz,
Florian Steinbächer

Detailed Proposals

Directors
Martin Reichert, Eva Schad, Alexander Schwarz

Project Architects
Martin Reichert, Eva Schad

Team
Janna Bunje, Adrian Dunham, Harald Eggers,
Annette Flohrschütz, Michael Freytag, Anke Fritzsch,
Isabelle Heide, Christoph Hesse, Christiane Melzer,
Franziska Rusch, Christian Stiller

Production Information

Directors
Martin Reichert, Eva Schad, Alexander Schwarz

Project Architects
Martin Reichert, Eva Schad

Team
Christiane Abel, Arnaud Bauman, Thomas Benk
(Historic Constructions), Johannes Bennke,
Daniela Bruns, Katja Buchholz, Nils Dallmann,
Florian Dirschedl, Maryla Duleba, Matthias Fiegl (ME),
Annette Flohrschütz, Michael Freytag (Team Leader
New Construction), Anke Fritzsch (Team Leader
Restoration), Katja Gursch, Anne Hengst,
Michael Kaune, Regine Krause, Paul Ludwig,
Martina Maire, Marcus Mathias, Werner Mayer-Biela,
Virginie Mommens, Harald Müller, Max Ott,
Peter Pfeiffer, Martina Pongratz, Robert Ritzmann,
Mariska Rohde, Franziska Rusch, Elke Saleina,
Sonja Sandberger, Antonia Schlegel, Gunnar Schmidt,
Lukas Schwind, Doreen Souradny, Annika Thiel,
Barbara Witt, Sebastian Wolf

Restoration Architect
Julian Harrap Architects: Julian Harrap,
Caroline Wilson

Consultant/Site Supervision
(Restoration)
Pro Denkmal GmbH: Uwe Bennke, Peter Besch,
Tom Bremen, Janna Bunje, Wolfgang Frey,
Ayten Güleryüz, Stefan Mayer, Martin Pomm,
Larissa Sabottka, Stefan Schiefl, Joachim Schröder,
Heiner Sommer, Claudia Vollmann

Quantity Surveyor
Nanna Fütterer for David Chipperfield Architects

Site Supervision
Lubic & Woehrlin GmbH for David Chipperfield
Architects: Corinna Becker, Evelyne Billo,
Markus Bondzio, Christoph Gläser, Hubert Greiner,
Monika Hagedorn, Mona Ibrahim, Gerda Lange,
Alexander Lubic, Michael Martin, Thomas Möbbeck,
Gottfried Paul (Chief Site Manager), Mathias Poleh,
Rolf Schneider, Dirk Schubert, Jirka Semecky-Overweg,
Tobias Strenge, Stefan Woehrlin, Inka Woschinik

Project Controlling
Ernst & Young Real Estate GmbH: Gerhard Kamolz,
Gerlinde Krüger (Project Manager), Alexandra Laugksch

Structural Engineer
Ingenieurgruppe Bauen: Prof. Gerhard Eisele
(Project Manager), Markus Filian, Sylvia Glomb,
Kerstin Gscheidle, Dorothea Rützel,
Stefanie Rosenberg, Kerstin Schmidt, Josef Seiler

Services Engineer
(Heating, Ventilation, Sanitary)
Jaeger, Mornhinweg+Partner Ingenieurgesellschaft:
Xavier Calvo (Project Manager), Ernst Göppel,
Volkmar Grossman, Andreas Koch, Hans-Ulrich Jäger,
Walter Ruschel

Services Engineer
(Electrical and Security)
Kunst und Museumsschutz Beratungs- &
Planungs-GmbH: Jörg Buchholz, Wolfgang Fuchs,
Jorg-Dieter Haack, Klaas Hemmen, Lutz Henske,
Wolfgang Liebert (Project Manager), Thorsten Schöne,
Dirk Pankau

Lighting Consultant
Kardorff Ingenieure Lichtplanung: Gabriele von Kardorff
(Project Manager), Volker von Kardorff, Stefan Krauel,
Katrin Söncksen, Iris Tegtbur

Building Physics
Ingenieurbüro Axel C. Rahn GmbH: Matthias Friedrich
(Project Manager), Michael Müller, Prof. Axel C. Rahn,
Thomas Riemenschneider

Landscape Architect
Levin Monsigny Landschaftsarchitekten: Nicolai Levin

Exhibition Design
architetto Michele de Lucchi S.r.L.: Michele de Lucchi,
Giovanna Latis, Sezgin Aksu, Heinz Jirout

Authors

David Chipperfield
David Chipperfield was born in London in 1953. He studied at Kingston School of Art and the Architectural Association in London. After graduating he worked at the practices of Douglas Stephen, Richard Rogers and Norman Foster. David Chipperfield Architects was established in 1984 and the practice currently has over 150 staff at its main offices in London, Berlin and Milan and representative office in Shanghai. The practice has won over 40 national and international competitions and many international awards and citations for design excellence, including RIBA, RFAC and AIA awards and the Stirling Prize 2007. David Chipperfield has taught and lectured extensively in Europe and the USA.

Kenneth Frampton
Kenneth Frampton was born in 1930 in Woking, UK. He is a British architect, critic, historian and the Ware Professor of Architecture at the Graduate School of Architecture, Planning and Preservation at Columbia University, New York. Frampton studied architecture at Guildford School of Art and the Architectural Association School of Architecture, London. Subsequently he worked in Israel, with Middlesex County Council and with Douglas Stephen and Partners (1961–66), during which time he was also a visiting tutor at the Royal College of Art (1961–64), tutor at the Architectural Association (1961–63) and Technical Editor of the journal *Architectural Design* (*AD*) (1962–65). Frampton has also taught at Princeton University (1966–71) and the Bartlett School of Architecture, London (1980). He has been a member of the faculty at Columbia University since 1972, and that same year he became a fellow of the Institute for Architecture and Urban Studies in New York and a co-founding editor of its magazine *Oppositions*. Frampton is well known for his writing on 20th-century architecture. His publications include *Modern Architecture: A Critical History* (1980; revised 1985, 1992 and 2007) and *Studies in Tectonic Culture* (1995).

Julian Harrap
Julian Harrap was born in Essex, UK, in 1942. He was educated in London under the tutelage of Sir Lesley Martin, Sir James Stirling and Colin St John Wilson. He established his own practice and has developed a particular knowledge and understanding of the design, technology and materials employed in the conservation of historic buildings and landscapes. Harrap has served on the historic buildings committees of conservation societies in the UK and has been involved in negotiating historic building legislation with the government. He regularly lectures on the theory and techniques of conservation repair throughout Europe and advises grant-giving agencies, such as the Getty Foundation and the National Heritage Lottery Board. Commissions include work on the Sir John Soane's Museum and Pitzhanger Manor. Harrap has advised the Royal Academy on historic building matters for a decade. Other commissions have included work for the National Trust and various charitable organisations. Harrap's portfolio includes work by Hawksmoor, Vanbrugh, Sir Charles Barry and John Nash.

Candida Höfer
Candida Höfer studied at the Kunstakademie Düsseldorf, first film with Ole John, then photography with Bernd Becher. Her work has been shown in museums including the Kunsthalle Basel, the Kunsthalle Berne, the Portikus, Franfurt am Main, and the Hamburger Kunsthalle. The artist has participated in group shows at the Museum of Modern Art, New York, the Power Plant, Toronto, the Kunsthaus Bregenz and the Museum Ludwig, Cologne. In 2002 Höfer participated in documenta 11. In 2003 she represented Germany at the Biennale in Venice (together with the late Martin Kippenberger). The artist lives in Cologne.

Jonathan Keates

Jonathan Keates was born in Paris in 1946. Educated at Bryanston and Magdalen College, Oxford, he teaches English at the City of London School. He is the author of a number of acclaimed biographies, including works on Händel, Purcell and Stendhal, as well as several travel books about Italy. He is also the author of the short story collection *Allegro Postillions* (1983), which won both the James Tait Black Memorial Prize and the Hawthornden Prize, and *Soon to Be a Major Motion Picture* (1997), as well as of two novels, *The Stranger's Gallery* (1987), set in 19th-century Italy, and *Smile Please* (2000), a comedy set in the gay community. Keates is a regular contributor to a number of newspapers and journals, including *The Sunday Telegraph* and the *Times Literary Supplement*. His latest work is a book of non-fiction, *The Siege of Venice* (2005), the story of Venice's last stand against its Austrian rulers in 1848/49.

Rik Nys

Rik Nys was born in Belgium in 1962. Trained as an architect at the Higher Institute of Arts and Sciences Department of Architecture Saint Lucas in Ghent, the Department of Architecture and Urban Planning at the Katholieke Universiteit Leuven and the Architectural Association in London, he has taught at the School of Architecture at Cambridge University and at London Metropolitan University. He has been Visiting Professor at the Federico II University in Naples and the Henry van de Velde Higher Institute of Architectural Sciences in Antwerp. His academic research, entitled 'Cultural Sustainability in Historic City Centers', focuses on case studies. Nys writes for art and architectural publications, and lectures on design, architecture and urbanism around Europe and Latin America. He has recently rejoined David Chipperfield Architects after working with Chipperfield for many years.

Joseph Rykwert

Joseph Rykwert was born in Warsaw, Poland, in 1926 and emigrated to England in 1939. Rykwert is an architectural historian who has published several books on architecture. He has taught at the University of Essex and the University of Cambridge. He is currently Paul Philippe Cret Professor of Architecture Emeritus and Professor of Art History at the University of Pennsylvania and has received a number of grants from the Graham Foundation to aid his work. Rykwert has also been a visiting scholar at various prestigious universities. He has taught a whole generation of architectural historians and theoreticians. Publications, among others: *On Adam's House in Paradise. The Idea of the Primitive Hut in Architectural History* (1981), *The Idea of a Town: The Anthropology of Urban Form in Rome, Italy, and The Ancient World* (1988), *The Dancing Column: On Order in Architecture* (1998). His most recent publication is *The Judicious Eye: Architecture Against the Other Arts* (2008).

Karsten Schubert

Karsten Schubert was born in West Berlin in 1961. He has worked as an artist's representative and London gallerist since the mid-1980s. Schubert is the main agent of Bridget Riley and Alison Wilding. His new gallery on Golden Square, which opened in 2007, is host to a focused exhibition programme that has shown Georg Baselitz, John Stezaker, Glenn Brown and many more leading artists. An accomplished writer, Schubert's first book, *The Curator's Egg,* has been translated into four languages. Schubert also runs the publishing imprint Ridinghouse, which produces 8 to 10 scholarly books a year.

Peter-Klaus Schuster

Peter-Klaus Schuster was born in Calw, Germany, in 1943. From 1962 to 1975 he studied art history, German literature and philosophy in Tübingen, Zurich, Frankfurt am Main and Göttingen. Between 1978 and 1981 he worked as conservator for fine and applied art from the 19th and 20th centuries at the Germanisches Nationalmuseum in Nuremberg. In parallel he lectured at the University of Regensburg. From 1981 to 1983, he was custodian for old masters at the Hamburger Kunsthalle. This was followed by the post of director of the department for 20th-century German art at the Bayerische Staatsgemäldesammlungen and a lectureship at Ludwig Maximilian University in Munich. From 1988 Schuster was head conservator and deputy director of the Nationalgalerie, before becoming director of the Alte Nationalgalerie from 1994 to 1997. During his time at the Berlin museums Schuster also taught at the Free University of Berlin. He then interrupted his activities in Berlin for a year in 1998/99 to assume the post of general director at the Bayerische Staatsgemäldesammlungen. From 1 August 1999 to 31 October 2008 he was general director of the Staatliche Museen and director of the Nationalgalerie in Berlin. He is currently guest scholar at the J. Paul Getty Museum.

Thomas Weski

Thomas Weski was born in Hanover in 1953. After studying visual communication at the University of Kassel, he worked as a freelance curator for the Siemens Arts Programme, Munich, and the photography gallery Spectrum in the Sprengel Museum Hanover. From 1992 to 2000 he was curator for photography and media at the Sprengel Museum Hanover, where he realised numerous exhibitions, mainly in the area of contemporary photography. As part of *EXPO 2000* he co-curated the highly regarded exhibition *How you look at it*, which brought together photography, painting and sculpture. In 2003 he was co-curator of the first photography exhibition held at the Tate Modern, *Cruel and Tender – Photography and the Real*, which after London moved to the Museum Ludwig, Cologne, where Weski was head curator from 2000 to 2003. In 2003 he then assumed the same post at the Haus der Kunst, Munich, where he realised solo exhibitions with Robert Adams, William Eggleston and Andreas Gursky as well as the thematic exhibition *ClickDoubleclick – das dokumentarische Moment*. Most recently active as deputy director, since mid-2009 Thomas Weski has held the endowed professorship 'Cultures of the Curatorial' at the Hochschule für Grafik und Buchkunst, Leipzig.

Wolfgang Wolters

Wolfgang Wolters was born in Frankfurt am Main in 1935. He studied art history and archaeology in Frankfurt, Freiburg and Munich before being appointed assistant to Ulrich Middeldorf at the Kunsthistorisches Institut in Florence (1966–70). Thereafter he was the first director of the Deutsches Studienzentrum in Venice (1971–74) and curator of monuments (section head) at the Bayerisches Landesamt für Denkmalpflege (1974–79). In 1977 he completed post-doctoral qualifications at Ludwig Maximilian University in Munich, before assuming a professorship at the Technical University of Berlin (1979–2001). Wolters was not only actively involved in preserving Venice in his capacity as vice president and program administrator of Save Venice Inc. (New York, until 1989), he has also written numerous books and articles on Venetian art and issues of historical conservation.

Index of photographs by Candida Höfer

Picture credits

2009 © David Chipperfield Architects, Candida Höfer,
authors and Verlag der Buchhandlung Walther König

Editors: Rik Nys and Martin Reichert for David Chipperfield Architects
Design: John Morgan, Michael Evidon and Daniel Chehade for John Morgan studio
Copyediting: Alison Smith, Jessica Strachan and Jennifer Taylor
Translation: Paul Bowman
Production: Printmanagement Plitt, Oberhausen

Published by
Verlag der Buchhandlung Walther König
Ehrenstr. 4, 50672 Köln
T +49 (0) 221 / 20 59 6-53
F +49 (0) 221 / 20 59 6-60
E verlag@buchhandlung-walther-koenig.de

The Deutsche Nationalbibliothek lists this publication
in the Deutsche Nationalbibliografie; detailed bibliographic
data are available at http://dnb.d-nb.de.

Printed in Germany

Distribution outside the United States and Canada,
Germany, Austria and Switzerland by
Thames and Hudson Ltd, London
www.thamesandhudson.com

Distribution in the United States and Canada by
D.A.P. / Distributed Art Publishers, Inc.
155 6th Avenue, 2nd Floor
New York, NY 10013
T +1 212-627-1999
F +1 212-627-9484
www.artbook.com

ISBN 978-3-86560-704-1